GHOSTS OF OLD SALEM, NORTH CAROLINA

G.T. MONTGOMERY

Haunted America

Published by Haunted America
A Division of The History Press
Charleston, SC 29403
www.historypress.net

First published 2014

ISBN 9781540223418

Library of Congress CIP data applied for.

Notice: The information in this book is true and complete to the best of our knowledge. It is offered without guarantee on the part of the author or The History Press. The author and The History Press disclaim all liability in connection with the use of this book.

*This book is dedicated to Dad and Mom, my loving parents,
and Genevieve, my loving wife.*

CONTENTS

CONTENTS

In Memoriam

This book is also dedicated to my grandmother Elizabeth Kennedy Simon Thomas, or as my cousins and I called her, "Libba." Libba passed away on Sunday, September 15, 2013, before I knew this project would come to pass, but I know she would have been proud to see me pursue it. Of all the people I have had in my life, Libba was one of the most influential in setting an example of what it means to appreciate literature. She was a true lover of books, as indicated by her varied and prolific collection of them, and I know she would have been thrilled to hear that I meant to add one of my own to her shelves.

I thought about Libba a fair amount during the composition of this book. I heard back from The History Press about moving forward with the project just six and a half weeks after Libba passed away, and thus, I could not help but have her on my mind. That said, there are a lot of elements in *Ghosts of Old Salem, North Carolina* that I know would have fascinated my grandmother.

Before attending Libba's funeral, we, the family, met that morning at the funeral home. This particular funeral home (Pearson's on Breckenridge Lane in Louisville, Kentucky) happened to be moments away from one of my grandmother's favorite establishments in the city, Plehn's Bakery. Plehn's is everything that a local bakery should be: every baked good is hand-crafted and fresh as can be; no matter what day or time you are there, it is likely you'll see somebody you know; and the service staff remembers who you are, even if you have been away a month or two. The bakery dates back nearly a century, having been established by Kuno Plehn, a native of Germany, in 1922.

When Libba heard that one of my many assignments as an employee of Old Salem Museums and Gardens (OSMG) was to assist in the baking of Winkler Bakery's many fine offerings, she was—so to speak—tickled. One specific detail that seemed to amuse her was the image of me shaping my hands into talon-like forms to cover unbaked sugar cake with divots, in which an indescribable, delicious mixture of butter, sugar and spices settles during the baking process. As Plehn's is in Louisville, so, too, is Winkler Bakery a must-stop for those who visit Old Salem.

Another fitting comparison is the fact that Winkler Bakery was established by an immigrant as well. In 1807, Swiss native Christian Winkler bought the building in which Winkler Bakery is still located today and began making the baked goods for which Old Salem is known. Many recipes used in the bakery today descended straight from those of Christian Winkler.

On our way from the funeral home to the church, we passed Seneca Park, one of several parks within Louisville named for a Native American tribe. It brought to mind a map of the United States that Libba had given me when I was a boy. Instead of showing fifty states, the country was broken down into areas showing where each Native American tribe once resided.

The map may have been an acquisition made during a trip she took in the latter part of her life in which she retraced, in part, the journey of Lewis and Clark. Her interest in history was so fervent that she took numerous photos for me of the exact sights Lewis and Clark had taken in along their journey and wrote down tidbits about their adventure. It was always a source of pride for her that, as we think of it here in Louisville, Lewis and Clark, in fact, started their journey across the west in Louisville. The two explorers did, after all, stop in Louisville to see Clark's brother, George Rodgers Clark, before moving west to St. Louis and formally starting their Jefferson-commissioned expedition.

That said, Libba found the story of Salem's Moravians to be a source of fascination, too. Like Lewis and Clark's trek, the migration of the Moravians halfway down the eastern seaboard into North Carolina was no small feat. While Old Salem now appears as a paragon of order and architecture, one can only imagine what a wild woodland it must have been when Salem's first settlers arrived.

Of course, an important part of Salem's establishment was the ability it lent the Moravian church to reach out to the Native Americans in the Piedmont area to share their Christian faith. Like the map Libba brought back for me, one wonders if the Moravians diagrammed the tribes around them in a similar way.

Not far from Seneca Park, our caravan then passed in front of an important landmark from my grandmother's life, the campus of the Ursuline Sisters of Louisville. Just like some of Salem's Moravian immigrants, the Ursuline sisters who established a Louisville presence were also natives of Germany. The sisters migrated to Kentucky to heed a call to be teachers at Louisville's St. Martin of Tours parish school. They first established a convent and boarding school in the same neighborhood as St. Martin, but as the community of sisters grew, as well as their commitment to Catholic education, the sisters started developing the campus in 1877 that our caravan would pass on the way to Libba's funeral.

The campus was a touching thing to drive by that morning because of the impact that the Ursulines had made in the life of my grandmother. Libba and my grandfather Frank had sent their children to school on the Ursuline campus, both to Sacred Heart Model School and Sacred Heart Academy, and had seen them achieve life milestones like their first Communion and confirmation there. Though I did not attend school on the campus, even I spent time there in my youth, taking piano lessons from an Ursuline sister seated by my side at an old piano.

Of course, the mission of the Moravians in Salem shows many similarities to that of the Ursulines. Granted, the Ursuline sisters were part of the Catholic Church from which the Moravians had broken away, but it is interesting to me the way that both groups intertwined their faith and education and how both pursuits were made priorities. Just as Sacred Heart Academy, the high school established by the Ursulines in 1877, is still an all-female school preparing young ladies for college, so, too, is Salem Academy in Old Salem. Libba's respect for faith, education and tradition as expressed in her support of the Ursuline sisters mirrored that same respect for those things as exhibited by the Moravians.

After passing the Ursuline campus, our procession continued down Lexington Road, and minutes later, we passed a significant symbol of Libba's interests in the world, the Antique Market at Distillery Commons. If there was a type of collecting that interested Libba as much as books, it was, without a doubt, collecting antiques.

My memories of visiting Libba as a child and experiencing all the unusual artifacts she had acquired through the years will always stay with me. Whether it was her display of glass julep glasses from Kentucky Derbies past, her array of dolls ranging from those in porcelain to those hand-sewn or her variety of furniture pieces like the miniature roll-top desk she once gifted to my older sister, everything in her home hearkened to a different era. Though my grandmother was a social person—not, perhaps, the loner sitting in a house full of dusty, moth-balled stuff that one might imagine—antiquing was, for her, a passion up until the end. From her, I learned the important lesson that items from the past can help tell the story of that time and place.

Needless to say, Old Salem's very mission corresponds to a focus on preservation, understanding the past and helping share history with new generations. The organization's Museum of Early Southern Decorative Arts (MESDA) especially reminded me of Libba. I know my grandmother would have appreciated each and every piece displayed in the museum. Though she was too frail to visit me in North Carolina during my years as an employee of Old Salem, I certainly shared MESDA with her from afar. Where some may have seen only old furniture, I know Libba would have seen artistry, craftsmanship and a form of creation made possible only by human hands.

Our last stop was the church, St. Martin of Tours Catholic Church on Shelby Street, just off of Broadway. As our procession approached the church's neighborhood, the narrow, pale green steeple of the building became visible over the roofs of the other buildings surrounding it. Exactly one block north of St. Martin's, another steeple stands, too: the one atop the first convent the Ursuline sisters built in 1859.

Inside St. Martin's one finds a beautiful church, a fact largely attributable to one of the best friends Libba made in her lifetime, Father Vernon Robertson. Father Robertson believed St. Martin's could remain a source of spirituality, beauty and peace even as the neighborhood around it deteriorated.

On either side of the church's altar, displayed in clear glass boxes for all the faithful to see, are the skeletons of two saints, St. Bonosa and St. Magnus. When I was a child and my family members on occasion found ourselves attending Mass there, I thought the skeletons were downright scary. I did not understand why human remains were on display or what about the bones made them so venerable. Now, however, when I see the skeletons, they look peaceful. There they rest, keeping an eye on the interior of the church, as they "wait in joyful hope for the coming of the Lord."

Old Salem, I think, is a bit like that. It is a place surrounded by death, whether it be God's Acre on its north end or the Stranger's Graveyard on its south end, but more often than not, it is not a spooky place to be. Rather, as the name suggests, it is a place of "peace," and the tombstones that one sees are a testament to the devoted souls who lived and worked there to make Salem thrive and be a place all would want to come.

May this book be an honor to the annals of Old Salem and, in the end, a tribute to the town and its history. I do not intend for it to discourage people from wanting to visit but, rather, hope it will help tell part of the story of an American treasure. I, for one, feel like my time at Old Salem shaped me for the better and enriched my knowledge of the world. Here is hoping it continues to do so for those who visit its streets, whether to hunt ghosts or seek sugar cake.

As for Libba, I like to believe she is, in some way, still watching over me. May this book—a combination of history, spirituality and storytelling—be a work that would make her proud. I know I owe my own love of history and reverence for the divine to the example Libba set in her life. I hope I give that example adequate due in the pages that follow.

PREFACE

In preparing to write this book, I came across a thin volume entitled *Ghosts of Salem and Other Tales*. In comparison to the age of Old Salem, the book is not that old: it was published in 2002 by the Moravian Archives. That said, after spending some time with the publication, I learned from its preface that a number of stories within the book had been recorded less recently. The basis for the publication, I discovered, came from the files of Adelaide L. Fries, specifically a file she listed as "Home-made Ghost Stories."

Fries, born in 1871, was a descendant of no less than Count Nicholas Ludwig Von Zinzendorf, the noble who provided safe haven for Moravians being persecuted early in the eighteenth century. She attended Salem College, from which she received both a bachelor of arts and master of arts degree. Fries used her education to pursue a study of the history of the Moravian Church and helped establish the Moravian Archives as they exist today. In 1911, just before turning forty, Fries was named the official archivist of the Moravian Church, Southern Province.

Nevertheless, during her forty-year tenure in the aforementioned position, Fries not only maintained church records but also set aside some time to write down the more mysterious side of Salem's history. Upon recording some of Salem's out-of-the-ordinary tales, she deposited them in her "Home-made Ghost Stories" file.

Though Fries passed away in 1949, fortunately, her file of "home-made" stories did not go undiscovered. C. Daniel Crews went on to become the chief archivist, and it was the assistant archivist with whom he worked,

Richard Starbuck, who stumbled on the collection among Fries's other work. Starbuck, intrigued by Fries's stories, formally compiled and supplemented them, thus creating the 2002 *Ghosts of Salem and Other Tales*.

Needless to say, without the work of Fries and Starbuck, this book would not have been possible. I would like to extend a special thank-you to Fries and Starbuck for taking the time to record the stories they did so that I and countless others could enjoy them. Without their efforts, some of Salem's most stirring stories may have been lost. I hope this compilation will inspire others as I was inspired by their compilation.

With regard to this collection, I should say: I have sought to present the reader tales common in and around the Old Salem historic district. That having been said, in spite of the work of those like Fries and Starbuck, some of the stories on which I stumbled lacked details and specifics. In addition to maintaining the essential integrity of the tales you will find within these pages, as I wrote, I also tried to add nuance where I felt it could be reasonably extrapolated. That said, as you read, please feel free to allow your imagination to do the same.

One last note: for those passages within the book taken from my personal experience, some names have been changed to protect the privacy of individuals.

ACKNOWLEDGEMENTS

I would first like to thank The History Press for providing me the opportunity to create this book and the entire team there who helped create this final product. I will always be grateful to Banks Smither, my commissioning editor, for his positive response to my book proposal and the steps he took to make the publication of *Ghosts of Old Salem, North Carolina* a reality. My thanks to Banks, as well, for answering my numerous questions throughout the process.

Thank you, too, to the many local writers who inspired me to pursue this project with the example of their books. The publication of their stories not only demonstrated that Winston-Salem and North Carolina have an abundance of tales to tell but also inspired me to spin some yarns, so to speak, of my own. Long before I ever lived or worked in North Carolina, I remember reading a volume my parents brought back to Kentucky after a visit to the Tarheel State—*North Carolina Ghosts and Legends* by Nancy Roberts. When reading that book as a boy, little did I know that I would go on to work in the very vicinity of the "Little Red Man" mentioned in Ms. Roberts's work. Better yet, I did not know that I would also get the opportunity to write a publication of my own, which—I hope—will stand on some bookshelf somewhere next to *North Carolina Ghosts and Legends*.

Thank you to Kathy Miller Hawkins and Miller Photography for providing my headshot. Thank you, also, to the team at Murphy's Camera for processing my film and working with me to meet submission requirements.

A tremendous thank-you to those organizations that provided me vintage images to include in the book. Without a doubt, the images shared by those organizations serve to bring the stories within these pages to life. A special thank-you to Molly G. Rawls, the photograph collection librarian at the Forsyth County Public Library, for going above and beyond to help me in a time of need. My appreciation, as well, to Gary Albert and the Photographic Services Office of Old Salem Museums and Gardens (OSMG). How could I have written a book about Old Salem without the aid of Old Salem Museums and Gardens?

On that note, a huge debt of gratitude to all my colleagues at Old Salem Museums and Gardens. Having worked with you nearly three years, I had the chance to experience firsthand your dedication to preserving Old Salem. I will always look back with fondness on my time at OSMG and will always cherish the months spent working with you. I hope my desire to honor the hard work you do year in and year out to make Old Salem an enriching experience for its visitors is reflected in these pages.

I would also like to thank all those along the way that encouraged me to pursue my writing. The excellent English teachers I had throughout my years as a student led me to major in English literature when I arrived in college and further devote myself to the written word. With regard to my years at Wake Forest, I am particularly grateful to Conor O'Callaghan and Vona Groarke. The time I spent in their poetry workshops was not only thoroughly enjoyable but also thoroughly educating. I will never forget their instruction to see the world with unique eyes.

Thank you, also, to the members of the Bill Bray Writers Group of Winston-Salem. Though my attendance to their meetings was inconsistent (to say the least), their passion for the craft of writing and their serious pursuit of publication encouraged me to pursue both. Needless to say, they were one of the first groups of people with whom I wanted to share news of *Ghosts of Old Salem, North Carolina*.

Thank you—of course!—to my family. To my grandparents; my four creative, inspiring sisters; and my always loving, always supportive parents: I would not be here without your presence in my life. Whether it be term papers you helped me proofread in high school, college applications for which you provided feedback or your words of encouragement at times of discouragement, I could not have created this work without your support. I am especially grateful for the creative environment in which I grew up. Whether it be the Chris Van Allsburg books I was read as a child, *Nutcracker* performances we attended each December, an unexpected visit to *The Royal*

Tenenbaums house in Harlem or after-dark ghost tours taken in Charleston or New Orleans, I am so thankful, Dad and Mom, for the encouragement of the imagination you have provided me.

Finally, thank you to my absolutely incredible wife, Genevieve. Your love and encouragement have been boundless. I think back to when we first started dating and you allowed me to try some of my poetry out on you—very brave! No less, there have been countless other times that you inspired me to pursue my dreams and encouraged me to stick with my writing, whether it be the storybook about Bruce (that I still owe you!), my posts to Examiner.com or this very book.

As I have pursued this project, I am so thankful for you tolerating my 5:00 a.m. alarms, my disappearances for hours at a time to sit in front of a computer and my general distractedness. Regardless, through it all, you showed me nothing but support, and without it, I could not have completed this manuscript. I am so lucky to have you by my side, and I am eternally grateful for all you do. I love you.

A LETTER FROM THE AUTHOR

Saturday, November 2, 2013

Today, as we say in the Catholic Church, is All Souls' Day. Thursday night's trick-or-treating is over, Halloween decorations are 75 percent off at the convenience store and, unlike yesterday (All Saints' Day), today is not a Holy Day of Obligation. Perhaps, though, the fact that today commemorates *all* those who have died, not just those who achieved the "St." before their names, makes it especially sacred. As inspiring as the saints are, I know there are many souls still seeking their heavenly home.

For those souls that seem destined to wander Earth, may this book help tell their tale. May acknowledging their restlessness in these pages somehow, in some way, help them on their path to peace. For those spirits within and without Old Salem, I offer up this prayer from the Mass:

Lord Jesus Christ,
you said to your apostles,
"I leave you peace,
my own peace I give to you."
Look not on our sins,
but on the faith of your Church,
and grant us the peace and unity
of your Kingdom,
where you live forever and ever.

Sincerely,
G.T. Montgomery

INTRODUCTION

As I set out to share Old Salem's best ghost tales, I am struck by how appropriate it is that I first started working in the historic town sometime around Halloween. I cannot recall much about my first day as an employee of Old Salem Museums and Gardens (the nonprofit organization that now owns, operates and preserves much of the colonial town), but I do remember the day I applied for the job.

I had seen a post on oldsalem.org advertising an open position for "Sales Associate, Retail Department." Though I had never worked a day of retail in my life, I had been raised to appreciate the importance of historic preservation, and the thought of working for a place with such a long, rich history appealed to me.

At the time—the autumn of 2009—I lived, relative to Old Salem, on the opposite side of the city. Whereas Old Salem is nestled on the south side of Winston-Salem's downtown central business district, I lived on the north side of the city, just above, as it falls on a map, Wake Forest University. In fact, I lived within walking distance of a different Moravian settlement—the Bethabara Historic District. As old as Old Salem is (it was established in 1766), Bethabara is even older, having been established in 1753.

One afternoon, I put on some pressed pants and an Oxford shirt and drove across town to fill out an application. When I entered Old Salem, as is the case for anyone who visits the historic district, it was like driving back in time to the eighteenth century. The building in which I was to apply, the Single Brothers' House, sat across from Old Salem's town square, looking every bit the same as it had when its last addition was completed in 1786. I knocked on one of its two wooden front doors and was greeted by a gentleman dressed from head-to-toe in garments straight out of 1800. He redirected me to the other wooden door, saying, "Sure, I can tell you where to go. Just walk down to the next door, let yourself in, walk up the stairs and a receptionist will be there who can help you."

After climbing the steep stairwell just inside the second door, I discovered that the receptionist had stepped out of the office. I stood in front of the reception desk at a loss for what to do, when a different gentleman found me standing there.

"Hi. Hello there. Anything I can help you with?" the man—dressed in modern garb but equal in friendliness to the guide I had met on the other side of the building—asked me. After I explained why I was there, the man looked around the office until he found a blank job application for me. Once I had application and pen in hand, he wished me luck, told me I could just set it on the desk and that I would hear back from them soon.

I mention this story to illustrate that—in spite of its penchant for spirit activity and unexplainable phenomena—Old Salem is also one of

Shadows fall across the Salem Moravian Graveyard in an image from the 1940s. *Courtesy of Forsyth County Public Library Photograph Collection.*

The Single Brothers' House is seen in this image from the 1940s. *Collection of Old Salem Museums and Gardens.*

the friendliest places one can visit. To provide a sense of what the larger atmosphere of Old Salem Museums and Gardens is like, I should note that the man who stopped what he was in the middle of doing to help me, I would later find out, was the chief financial officer of the entire $7.5 million organization. That, my very first experience at Old Salem, was a welcoming one, and the two separate tenures I ultimately worked there would provide me many equally pleasant memories.

That having been said, as friendly as the administration, management and co-workers with whom I worked at Old Salem were, the historic district is indeed a very old place, and as a result, there is no question that the Moravian town has seen a wide variety of people pass through since it was first established. I had not been an employee long when I first started hearing tales of certain people who had refused to leave the grounds of Old Salem, even after death.

The first building in which I worked after getting hired by OSMG was a former Coca-Cola bottling plant constructed in 1925 and acquired by Old Salem in 1986. Most folks would not recognize it as part of the living history museum. For one, it sits two blocks west of the historic district, and for another, its architecture does not quite correspond with that of traditional Moravian structures. Unlike the buildings in Old Salem proper with arches over doorways and cupolas atop roofs, the Distribution Center (as it is known) appears as a wide, one-story brick façade with a large white loading-bay door next to a standard hunter-green metal door. On the shorter green door hangs a small rectangular sign with Old Salem's logo indicating the building's affiliation with OSMG's older, more historic buildings half a mile away.

The first ghost story I heard at Old Salem was not that of the "Little Red Man" or the "cold spot" but rather a personal recollection one of my co-workers shared with me, and it so happened that it took place in the Distribution Center. Here is how she relayed the tale to me:

This particular co-worker, Caitlin, was working in the Distribution Center late one night. The rest of the crew had gone home for the evening, and she found herself alone in the ten-thousand-square-foot warehouse. The warehouse, in fact, is a combination of multiple components: on one side of a door is an office space with various desks, cubicles, filing cabinets and the like. On the other side of the same door, however, is the warehouse itself, an area that includes a chilled room for storing the multitudinous beeswax candles sold each year, a standard storage area for keeping various supplies and materials and a shipping area used to process online orders.

Whereas I initially worked in the shipping area, Caitlin's position was such that she worked at one of the desks in the office space. The restrooms for the Distribution Center, however, are located in the center of the building, necessitating that those in the office pass by the shipping area to get to them.

That night, Caitlin sat working at her desk when she thought she heard something in the warehouse. Her fingers paused over her keyboard, and she listened for the noise to repeat itself.

"Hello? Anybody out there?" she hollered toward the warehouse on the other side of the office door. She thought maybe someone else had come in to finish up some work or prepare for the next day, but there was no answer. She listened another moment to see if the sound would occur again, but other than the gentle whir of her computer, there was nothing to be heard. She looked back at her computer screen and tried to resume her work, but as soon as she started typing, she paused again. She realized she would not be able to concentrate on her work until she investigated the inexplicable noise from the warehouse.

She went to the door separating the office from the warehouse and pulled on its brass knob. As she stepped out of the office, she did not hear anything else unusual but was struck by the sight of something unexplainable. Just a few yards in front of her, a large plume of white mist floated in the air. Unlike smoke or steam, however, the mist did not rise into the rafters of the warehouse but maintained a distinct form, like gnats that maintain an undulating sphere as they travel the air on a summer night.

Caitlin's experience, however, grew stranger. The white mist then began to drift across the warehouse. It did not dissipate or thin as it moved but held together as it wandered through the still air of the warehouse. The apparition floated from the metal racks at the south end of the warehouse, past the white van parked in the loading dock, in front of the shipping area with its preassembled boxes, and then moved down the dim hallway that led to the building's restrooms.

Caitlin, transfixed, had followed the movement of the plume with her eyes, but when it turned the corner into the hallway, she lost sight of it. Keeping her eyes trained on the last spot she had been able to see the cloud of mist, she moved across the warehouse herself, but when she got to the hallway, there was no sign of it in the corridor.

The strange sight was too unusual not to pursue further. Caitlin decided she had to see if she could find out what had happened to the apparition. She took a few steps into the hall and found herself standing in front of the narrow door that led into the ladies' room. She pushed open the door and flicked on the dim overhead light, but nothing appeared out of the ordinary. A small drip escaped from the faucet on the sink, and Caitlin caught a glimpse of herself in the mirror over the sink, but there was no mist to be seen.

The next step would be to check the men's room. She reached to turn off the light and exit the women's room, but before she could, a toilet flushed behind one of the two closed stall doors. Caitlin repeated the same questions she had asked earlier, directing them at the drab beige paint on the front of the stall door.

"Hello?" she asked. "Anybody in there?" No reply. She asked again but louder the second time, "Hello? Is somebody in there?" Yet, again, there was no response. Taking two steps forward, Caitlin extended her arm and pushed open the door on the stall, but unexplainably, there was no one inside who could have done the flushing.

~

As I got to know all my co-workers better, I learned that it was not an uncommon occurrence for OSMG employees to experience things out of the normal. Another one of my colleagues, Hattie, relayed to me a consistent happening that took place in the historic district's J. Blum House.

The Blum House, a two-story home with white siding, sits on Main Street just north of the Tavern in Old Salem restaurant. The name comes from the original owner of the home, John Christian Blum, who had the home built in 1815. If the name sounds familiar, it could be its connection to *Blum's Farmer's and Planter's Almanac*, a publication established by John Blum that is still printed each year.

Before pursuing printing, Blum attempted both tavern keeping and working as an agent for Cape Fear Bank, but both ventures proved poor fits. After making the switch to the printing trade, Blum began publishing his almanac in 1828, which turned out to be quite popular in the agricultural state of North Carolina.

Because the Blum House had originally been the home of Salem's printer, it was, therefore, appropriate that for a number of years Old Salem Museums and Gardens utilized the building as a stationery shop. The building now serves solely as an exhibit for visitors, and any evidence of its retail past is no longer present. However, while it was a shop, it did not fail to yield some strange occurrences, which Hattie experienced firsthand.

On multiple occasions, Hattie saw from the corner of her eye someone ascending the wooden steps that led to the second floor. The second floor, however, was not open to the public. Hattie, committed to keeping track of customers and merchandise, would hurry up the steps to redirect the wandering visitor back to the first floor, only to discover nobody was on the second level. Little did I know that, like Hattie, after I worked at Old Salem long enough, I would have a supernatural experience of my own.

I had been working for OSMG for a number of months and had gotten to the point that I could close up the store in which I worked on my own. Granted, it was almost never necessary because those of us scheduled to work up until closing time usually made a joint effort of shutting down the

An aerial photograph from the 1930s showing Salem Cemetery in the lower right-hand corner with God's Acre and the Old Salem historic district to the west. *Courtesy of Forsyth County Public Library Photograph Collection.*

store, which largely consisted of turning off lights, switching off lamps and making sure all the doors were locked. Every so often, however, my fellow co-workers would have to leave right at 5:00 p.m. either to make a dinner date or meet a friend, and I would be left alone to execute the closing process.

One evening, I found myself in that very situation. By the time the last customers made their way out the door, my co-workers got on their way and I got the many lamps on display switched off, it was almost 6:00 p.m.—that time of day when the sun was just setting and the interior of the building was starting to darken. The day's final rays of sun stretched through the western windows of the shop, illuminating the glass Moravian stars hanging there.

Before I could leave though, I would first have to check the second floor and, once again, cut off any lights left burning. Unlike the first floor, however, which is laid out as one wide shopping area, the second floor is a combination of many different rooms. At the top of the stairs leading up to the second floor is a small room that is also part of the store and thus used to display merchandise. Beyond that are a few offices used by OSMG's Education Department, and at the very back of the second level sits a good-sized closet.

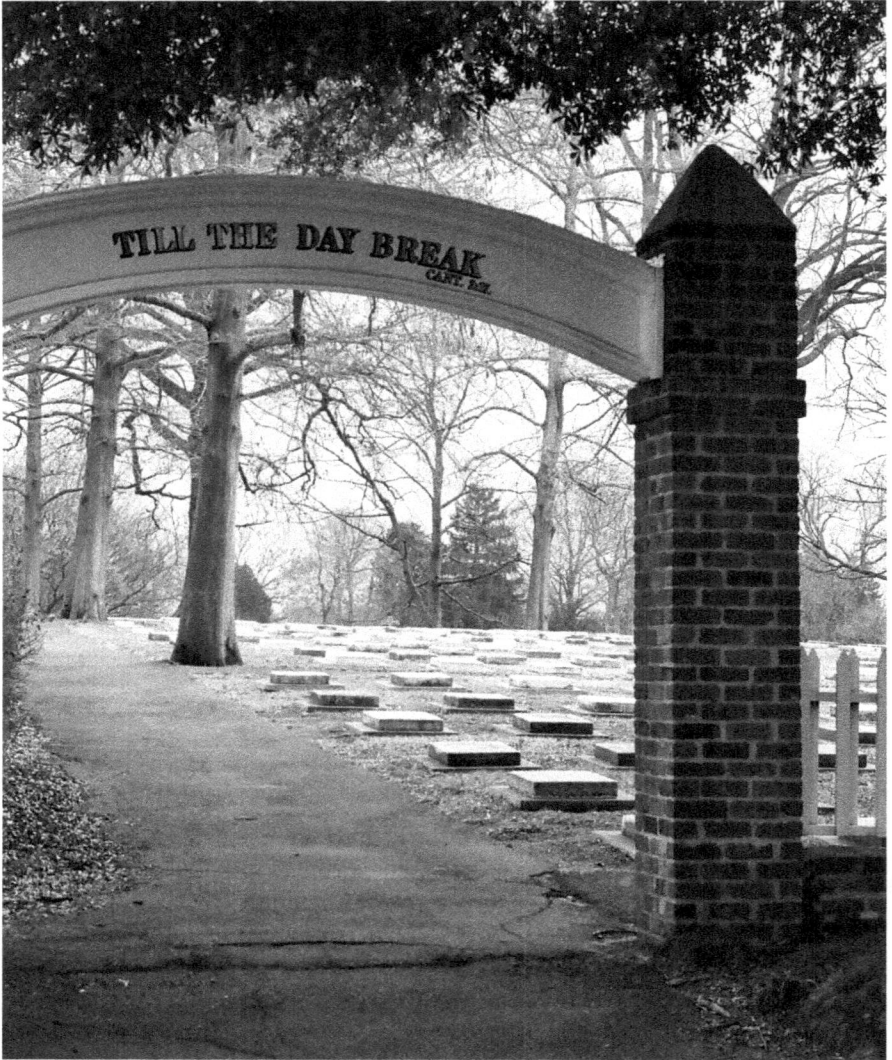

A path off of Cedar Avenue leads into God's Acre. *Photograph by G. T. Montgomery.*

I don't know what function the closet served when the building was first built, but knowing the penchant for efficiency Old Salem's Moravian settlers had, it surely had not always been a closet. At some point, however, the room had been converted to a storage space, as had the room below it and yet another room two floors below it in the basement. Furthermore, at some point in time the decision had been made to connect the three large closets with a modern dumbwaiter to help move things from one floor to another.

In spite of its availability, though, my co-workers and I never saw the necessity of the machine. Had we been moving encyclopedias from floor to floor, for example, it would have been a great benefit to us, but for the most part, none of the merchandise we handled required the small elevator to move it. As a result, the square openings cut in the wall for loading and unloading the dumbwaiter were almost always covered up by unused display fixtures, out-of-season decorations or backstock of our most popular products of which we always wanted large reserves. Consequently, the dumbwaiter was never used, until, that is, the night I closed alone.

I made my way to the storage room behind the offices of the educators to make sure everything was in order and that the lights were off in there as well. Yet when I opened the door to the closet, I could not help but notice a couple of candles that had rolled off the end of a table. As I made my way across the storage space to pick up the candles, I did not touch the dumbwaiter or any of its controls in any way. In fact, I was not even close enough to the machine that I could have brushed up against it unknowingly.

Regardless, as I stood there alone in the room and alone in the whole building, a mechanical whirring began emanating from within the dumbwaiter shaft. A moment later, there was a loud *ding*, the half dollar–sized "CAR HERE" light clicked on and the car of the dumbwaiter lurched to a stop behind the metal door. I was, to say the least, startled, but I felt compelled to see what might be in the out-of-use dumbwaiter. I walked to the back wall of the room, grasped the thin metal handle and lifted open the door. The machine's car, it turned out, was empty. Though I no longer live in Winston-Salem and may never lay eyes on that dumbwaiter again, I will always wonder who sent it traveling through the building's walls that night and what delivery I was supposed to receive.

PART I
AN INTRODUCTION TO OLD SALEM

CHAPTER 1

OLD SALEM, NORTH CAROLINA, VERSUS SALEM, MASSACHUSETTS

In the interest of full disclosure, I do want to clarify one thing from the outset of this book. In January 1692, Dr. William Griggs of Salem, Massachusetts, was summoned to examine both the daughter and niece of a local minister, Reverend Samuel Parris. The girls had fallen ill, and their health failed to improve on its own. Instead of providing a simple remedy, however, Dr. Griggs diagnosed the girls as being "bewitched."

The diagnosis would prove to instigate a dark period of time in American history known today as the Salem witch trials. At that time in Massachusetts, the authorities maintained a strong belief in God, not to mention a healthy fear of Satan, and—as history would tell—the combination of those beliefs would claim several lives. Practicing witchcraft was considered a capital offense, and those found guilty were not spared: in total, nineteen men and women were hanged, while several others died in prison awaiting their punishment. When the hysteria subsided, the town of Salem, Massachusetts, would never be the same. Indeed, to this day, the town still serves as a lure to Halloween enthusiasts, either seeking to find new bewitched souls or, perhaps, the souls of those executed at the hands of hysteric fanatics.

That having been mentioned, the Salem covered in this book is not *that* Salem. Rather, the "Old Salem" mentioned time and again in the pages to come refers to the colonial town established by Moravian missionaries in northwest North Carolina. The Salem covered in this book has no history of witchcraft.

An iron cross marks a plot in Salem Cemetery. *Photograph by G.T. Montgomery.*

To avoid any further confusion, it may also be helpful to mention that in addition to Old Salem in Forsyth County, North Carolina, there is also a town in Burke County, North Carolina, called Salem and a town in Union County, North Carolina, called New Salem. As best can be determined, the latter two communities also lack histories of witchcraft.

CHAPTER 2
A BRIEF HISTORY OF THE TOWN

The region of Moravia is located far from northwest North Carolina: the area occupies central and eastern Czech Republic. Like various other Protestant groups in Europe, Moravia's Protestant sect (called the Moravians) experienced persecution for their religion, and by the start of 1792, a group of the Unitas Fratrum, as they called themselves, had made their way to Pennsylvania and founded the town of Bethlehem.

It was from Bethlehem, Pennsylvania, that a select group of Moravians made a journey south into North Carolina, establishing a number of communities in the vicinity of present-day Winston-Salem. The first was Bethabara in 1753, the second was Bethania in 1759 and the third was Salem in 1766. Before the Moravian settlers arrived, the land where Old Salem now stands was undeveloped wilderness.

Once established, Salem flourished. It came to serve as the central hub on which other nearby Moravian settlements relied. Settlers began practicing a number of trades from within Salem, and the town developed a reputation as a source of food, tools and other essentials needed by those living in the area. The engineering ability of the Moravians was also unquestionable, as their buildings withstood not only the foundational years of Salem but, in fact, still stand in place to this day.

In that the Moravians also meant Salem to be an outpost for their missionaries, it is no surprise that they chose a biblical name for their town. "Salem" first appears in the Bible at Genesis 14:18: "And King Melchizedek of Salem brought out bread and wine; he was priest of God Most High."

Many, though, consider the name Salem to be a variation of "Jerusalem," which is, of course, found throughout the Bible, including the final book, Revelation. The term "Salem" itself derives from the Hebrew and Arabic words "shalom" and "salaam," respectively. One can extrapolate that Salem's founders must have been quite content with their new settlement for "Salem," in fact, means "peace."

By 1913, both Salem and its neighboring town just to the north, Winston, which was founded in 1849, had grown substantially to the point that the distinct communities had started growing into each other. As a result, on May 9, 1913, the merger of the two towns went into effect, and the resulting city was first called Winston-Salem.

As for the name "Winston," it is has decidedly more American roots: the town was named to honor one of the very men who helped the American colonies break away from British rule: Colonel Joseph Winston. Though not a native of North Carolina (he was born in 1746 in Louisa County, Virginia), Joseph Winston would go on to make a lasting impression on the people of the Tarheel State.

After the Revolutionary War broke out in 1775, Winston became a major in the Continental army. It was during the war that then-Major Winston led troops in two pivotal battles in the North Carolina area: firstly, the Battle of Kings Mountain, just south of the North Carolina border in 1780, and secondly, the Battle of Guildford Courthouse in Guildford County in 1781. The former was a clear victory for the Continental army, but it was the latter that—though a loss for the colonists—helped shift momentum against the British.

After defeat at the Battle of Guildford Courthouse, Major General Nathanael Greene (after whom Greensboro, North Carolina, was named) of the Continental army then moved his troops into South Carolina and subsequently undid British military control in the southern colonies. Meanwhile, British commander lieutenant general Charles Cornwallis, the victor at the battle in Guildford County, moved his troops north into Virginia, the place at which he would ultimately surrender to George Washington.

In 1849, Forsyth County, North Carolina, was formed out of land formerly belonging to Stokes County (now Forsyth County's neighbor to the north). At first, the county seat of Forsyth County was simply known as "the county town," but soon thereafter, the name was changed to Winston in tribute to Joseph Winston and his efforts to help establish America's independence. On April 21, 1815, Colonel Winston died in Germanton,

The tombs of Salem Cemetery as seen through the trees. *Collection of Old Salem Museums and Gardens*.

North Carolina, just thirteen miles north of the town (and subsequent city) that would come to bear his name.

Ironically, whereas the town of Winston was named to honor a man who fought to turn back British troops from American soil, the name "Carolina," in fact, was a tribute to the king of England at the time of its establishment, Charles I. King Charles I actually provided the original land grant in 1629 that would later become the state of North Carolina. The colony that was established on that land was called Carolina in a nod to the Latin form of Charles's name, "Carolus." Then, in 1729, the colony of Carolina was split into two—an upper Carolina and a lower Carolina, or, as we say to this day, North Carolina and South Carolina. In spite of its name having been initially intended to pay homage to one of Britain's kings, when North Carolina was formally accepted as a member of the United States of America in 1789, the name stayed the same.

Today, the seal of the City of Winston-Salem still showcases pictorial likenesses of the two towns that came together to create the "Twin City." It also contains the Latin motto "*Urbs Condita Adiuvando*," which translates into English as "a city founded on cooperation." The fact that one town was named to reflect the heritage of its pacifism-practicing Christian founders and the other to honor the heroism of a military commander, and that the resulting city is still solidly united one hundred years later, is a true testament to cooperation indeed.

CHAPTER 3

WHERE TO BEGIN A VISIT

For those who have never been to Old Salem, it may seem a bit unclear where to begin a visit since the attraction does span the breadth of an entire town. To be sure, there is no right or wrong answer: for some, a visit to Old Salem means nothing more than a stroll down its sidewalks, and for others, it entails touring every available exhibit. For yet another segment of the population, a visit to Old Salem can be built entirely on stopping in Winkler Bakery for fresh bread or sugar cake.

A great first stop for anyone interested in learning more about Old Salem is the Old Salem Visitor Center located at 900 Old Salem Road (not to be confused with the Winston-Salem Visitor Center at 200 Brookstown Avenue). Though the building in which it is located is much newer than most of the structures in Old Salem, the Visitor Center is not any less focused on presenting the history of the town.

As soon as one enters the Visitor Center, one is met with history: a larger-than-life portrait of Bishop August G. Spangenberg, who led the state's first Moravians from Pennsylvania to North Carolina to survey the land, hangs smiling at all those who enter the building. The portrait of Spangenberg (who went on to become bishop of all of North America's Moravian congregation in 1744) is one of thirty-five floor-to-ceiling wall displays inside the Visitor Center that narrate Old Salem's evolution and highlight key figures from its past. The pictures and text are a great introduction to many aspects of Old Salem, including its connection to the Moravian Church, the various trades that thrived in the town and the people who lived in the Moravian settlement.

The final of these wall displays hangs by the building's southernmost entrance and features a depiction of President George Washington, who not only visited Salem in 1791 but also spent two nights in its tavern.

Being a modern building with modern technology, the Visitor Center also utilizes film to introduce Old Salem to newcomers. Approximately every ten minutes, a short video plays for visitors on a large screen in the center of the building. The video provides a brief explanation of the town's origins and covers some of the various still-preserved buildings that define the historic district. For those with even more curious minds, the building also houses a bookstore stocked with numerous titles about Salem history, the Moravians and the area that surrounds present-day Winston-Salem. In addition to the film and the books, the Visitor Center is home to the Old Salem Welcome Desk, at which knowledgeable staffers answer countless questions each day about Old Salem, its history and its current offerings. At the Welcome Desk, visitors can also pick up brochures, receive maps and purchase tickets and memberships.

In spite of its modern trappings, however, the Visitor Center does shelter one particularly precious item from history: the world's largest surviving "Tannenburg Organ," one made by the Pennsylvania organ builder David Tannenburg. The massive organ of white-painted wood and gold metal trim was first installed in Old Salem's Home Moravian Church in 1799 but was dismantled in 1910. According to oldsalem.org, though the organ does still belong to Home Moravian Church, the experts at Old Salem Museums and Gardens oversaw the fifteen-year restoration of the majestic instrument. After restoration, the organ was then reinstalled, but this time within the James A. Gray Auditorium inside the Old Salem Visitor Center. There the organ resides (in a carefully climate-controlled environment), and for no charge—admission to the Visitor Center is free—the public can view a great treasure from Salem's past.

The Visitor Center is also a draw for many local residents and visiting guests, alike, in that it serves as a home to the Old Salem Candy Shop. The latter is certainly a popular attraction where visitors can find handmade fudge being poured, fresh popcorn being tumbled in caramel and, with luck, authentic Moravian cookies being sampled. Though a late addition to the array of buildings at Old Salem, it is not difficult to see why the Visitor Center is a logical starting point for those new to the historic town.

PART II
HAUNTINGS IN THE HISTORIC DISTRICT

CHAPTER 4

UPON ENTERING OLD SALEM

As one walks south on Church Street in Winston-Salem, moving from the downtown central business district toward Old Salem, there is a house with a black rubber rat lashed to the handrail leading up its front steps. Standing on the sidewalk in front of that house, one can see the northernmost boundary of Old Salem. One can see the stone pillars and the wrought-iron gate that mark the entrance to the so-called Cedar Avenue, a scenic sidewalk so named because of the dozens of ruddy-trunked, green-capped cedars that line it. Though Cedar Avenue is charming, something about passing the black rat suggests a sinister quality afoot as well.

One might convince one's self, however, that the rat is just a fluke. It is, after all, just a rubber toy. One could argue the prop is nothing more than a Halloween decoration that never got taken down before the colder, more blustery winter months set in for the season. Besides, the name of the street on which the house sits is "Church Street"—certainly such a name is indicative of a place more holy than it is sinister. One, thus, continues on toward Cedar Avenue and the quaint, historic town of Old Salem.

Before entering Old Salem, though, one comes to the intersection of Church Street and Cemetery Street. Crossing a road named for the graveyard it hems in also elicits a twinge of unease. On the other side of Cemetery Street, one discovers that the antique iron gate between the stone pillars, in fact, not only marks the entrance to Cedar Avenue but also the entrance to the Salem Moravian Graveyard.

A heavy chain keeps a tomb door in Salem Cemetery from coming open. *Photograph by G.T. Montgomery.*

Right: A street sign foretells Old Salem's dual nature as quaint but spooky. *Photograph by G.T. Montgomery.*

Below: A lock and chain on the gate into the Salem Moravian Graveyard. Is it meant to keep spirits from wandering into Old Salem's streets? *Photograph by G.T. Montgomery.*

The top of the iron gate is graced with a small heart, but below the heart—about a foot down—the gate is wrapped with a thick chain snapped together with a heavy, weathered lock. As scenic and serene as Cedar Avenue is, one cannot help but wonder what purpose the lock and chain serve. Are they, perhaps, an attempt to keep in the restless spirits of Old Salem? Continue walking, and you will find that some spirits cannot be shackled.

CHAPTER 5
CHILL OF A CHILD

The cemetery on the other side of the chained gate, as is a tradition in the Moravian Church, is more often called "God's Acre." The name God's Acre comes from the ancient German designation of "Gottesacker," which, translated into English, means "Field of God." The Moravians who settled Salem began laying to rest fellow members of their congregation in God's Acre in 1771.

As noted by findagrave.com, the Salem Moravian Graveyard is also called at times the "City of the Equal Dead" in that its tombstones "are all flat and are approximately the same size," and thus no person's headstone calls more attention to itself than does another. Moravian graveyards are also unique in that the faithful departed are laid to rest by "choir," rather than by family, with one's "choir" being determined by gender and marital status instead of parents or spouse. Findagrave.com describes the choir system in this way: "[M]arried [men] are buried in a choir and married [women] in another, [whilst] single [men] and single [women] are buried likewise; children are buried together in a [separate choir]."

One would think that a place labeled the "City of the Equal Dead" would be rife with stories of restless spirits. The first spirit one encounters at Old Salem's northern end, however, is just *beyond* God's Acre. For those who choose to follow Cedar Avenue down the length of the cemetery, they may find a distinct chill waiting at the other end.

On the other side of God's Acre, Cedar Avenue becomes Church Street once again. The street takes its name from Home Moravian Church, which

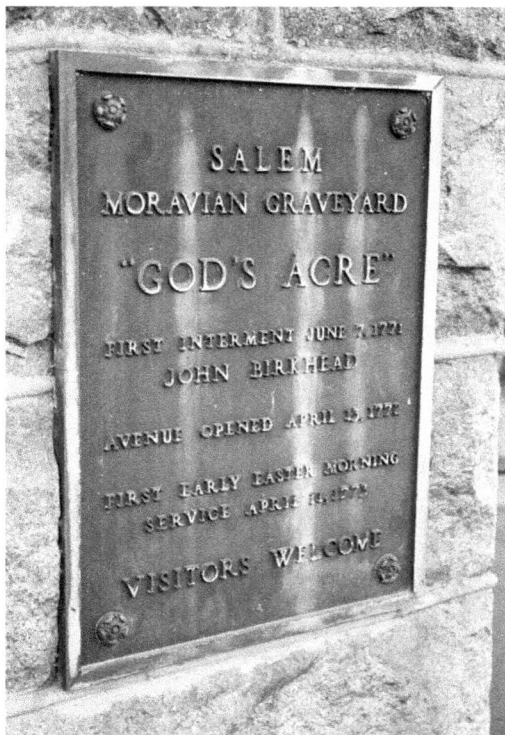

Left: A plaque affixed to one of the stone pillars that frame the entrance to God's Acre. *Photograph by G.T. Montgomery*.

Below: An image of the flat tombstones from the so-called City of the Equal Dead. *Photograph by G.T. Montgomery*.

A picture looking south shows Cedar Avenue on the western edge of God's Acre. *Photograph by G.T. Montgomery.*

was established on November 13, 1771, just five years after the Moravians began settling Old Salem. As to be expected, the church building, completed in 1800, sits directly on the street. Before arriving at the church, however, one first crosses Bank Street, and it is there that one might experience what has come to be known as Old Salem's "cold spot."

It was a beautiful winter morning in North Carolina. The sky was a bright blue, white clouds drifted by overhead and though the sun had risen and was shining, a fresh snow from the previous night covered everything. Businesses were closed, school was cancelled and across the city people stayed in their homes and waited for the frozen precipitation to melt.

Conversely, David, seven years old at the time, relished the opportunity to go outside and enjoy the winter weather. Unlike Pennsylvania, from whence Salem's original Moravian settlers had come, snow occurs infrequently in North Carolina's Piedmont region. David knew that if he and his friends wanted to go sledding, they needed to get outside as early as possible before the snow could melt. He also knew just the hill down which they could slide: the incline starting at the corner of Bank and Church Streets, emptying out at the corner of Salt and Church.

The boys grabbed anything they could find that seemed like it would glide over the snowy surface. Some of them had pieces of thin metal, some of them had thick swatches of cardboard, but David happened to have an actual sled. Though he did not get to use it every winter, when the occasion did arrive, his possession of the sled made him all the more popular with the other kids in the neighborhood.

David, of course, was willing to share the sled, but he did have one stipulation that, in his opinion, was reasonable: he insisted that he get the first trip down the hill before he would let any of his friends borrow the toy. As it would happen, that stipulation would spell doom for David.

As he stood at the corner of Bank and Church Streets and prepared himself for the inaugural run of the day, what David did not realize was

A marker identifies the final resting place of a child in the Strangers' Graveyard, long since paved over with a brick walkway. *Photograph by G.T. Montgomery*.

that below the snow on the surface, there was a layer of ice. Though David expected it to take a few runs to cut a smooth path down the hill and, ultimately, get some speed going, it would soon be evident that no such process was necessary.

With the sun rising and, perhaps, the temperature with it, David's friends urged him to stop stalling and initiate the morning of sledding. In response, he tugged on the bottom of both his mittens and adjusted his hat to make sure his ears were covered. He set the sled on the ground, boarded it and, with a shove of his feet, started down the hill.

In an instant, he noticed the icy cover over Bank Street covered by the thin layer of snow on the surface. The sled was moving much faster than he anticipated, and any slight attempt to steer threatened to send the sled veering to the left or right. As a consequence, David's strategy for mastering the Bank Street hill quickly devolved to keeping his head down, holding on tight and hoping to avoid a wipeout.

David, however, also lacked one other piece of key information: though the snow had shut down *most* of the city, one service it had not interrupted was that of the streetcar. Though David and the other neighborhood youths knew well that the streetcar traversed up and down the length of Main Street, they had assumed that the snowfall had cancelled the mass transit service just as it had interrupted everything else that day. Complicating matters was the fact that while standing at the top of the Bank Street hill, the kids were blind to traffic moving north on Main Street, including that of streetcars.

The timing could not have been worse. Still aboard his sled, David flew into the intersection of Bank and Main at the exact moment the streetcar attempted to cross Bank Street. For the rest of their lives, David's friends at the top of the hill would never forget the sickening sound of the impact or the horror of the sight as the streetcar dragged David a number of yards before the streetcar operator, John Ebert, could bring it to a stop. Though David held on long enough to get to the hospital, by the end of the day, he was dead.

In spite of the tragedy, once the scene was cleared, Bank Street reopened. The snow melted, weeks passed, the days lengthened and the residents of Salem believed they could put winter and its tragic incident behind them.

Yet as summer arrived and the weather grew warmer, there was one specific spot within the town that, somehow, stayed the same temperature all the time: cold. As men, women and children alike strolled along the sidewalks of the town, they all noticed that when they walked the stretch of Bank Street in between Church and Main, they were hit with an unnatural

The corner of Bank Street and Main Street where Salem's horrific streetcar accident took place. *Courtesy of Forsyth County Public Library Photograph Collection.*

A faded sign marks the Bank Street hill where young David lost his life. *Photograph by G. T. Montgomery.*

A picture from the 1940s captures the façade of Old Salem's Belo House, which overlooks Bank Street's cold spot. *Courtesy of Forsyth County Public Library Photograph Collection.*

chill. Then they made the connection: the cold spot that everyone continued to experience happened to mark the very place young David slid past before his horrifying collision with the streetcar.

To this day, it is not unusual to feel a sudden chill when you turn east off of Main Street and make your way up the Bank Street hill. Turn right again onto Church Street and the chill will have passed, but an eerie feeling may linger. One thing remains to be seen: is Old Salem's cold spot a reminder of the cold, wintery day on which David died, or rather, is it David himself, his spirit keeping eternal watch over the hillside on which he met his end?

CHAPTER **6**

LINGERING OF THE "LITTLE RED MAN"

Just one block south of the intersection where young David met his untimely death stands the Single Brothers' House. As the name suggests, the building was occupied by those men who were old enough to move out from their parents' homes but not yet married and ready to establish homes of their own.

The Single Brothers' House, as it stands today, is one of Old Salem's most unique buildings in that it is a union of two distinct styles. Initially, the Moravians completed construction on the lodging by the end of 1769, utilizing a half-timbered construction, a combination of thick, solid timbers filled in with brickwork. However, within the next decade and a half, the town of Salem continued to grow, and it soon became evident that either a second Single Brothers' House would have to be erected or the existing one would need expansion. As reflected in the building's current façade, the community opted for the latter and in 1786 extended the original Single Brothers' House to the south with an all-brick addition, consequently doubling the amount of lodging for the town's single men.

Andreas Kresmer was one such young man. At age thirty-three, he was still single and, thus, lodging and working with all the other men in the Single Brothers' House. Kresmer, though, would not live to see age thirty-four. Furthermore, while the name Andreas Kresmer would fade into history, a new name would emerge for the young man from the Single Brothers' House: the "Little Red Man."

It was an odd decision. It was Saturday night on March 25, 1786, and Salem's evening worship service had come to an end. Yet, for some reason, the men living in the Single Brothers' House were restless after the service of prayer and song. Perhaps it was the fact that spring seemed to have finally arrived, or it was the rousing sermon the minister had given in the worship service. Whatever it was, there was a general consensus within the Single Brothers' House that it was too early to retire for the day. Then one of the young men had a suggestion:

"Anyone want to work on the cellar?" It was the biggest project the men of the house wanted to complete before summer's arrival—the excavation of a cellar for their home. They had put it off until spring, thinking that warmer temperatures would make for softer soil and thus easier digging. Though the digging still did not come easy, March had brought with it warmer temperatures, and with Easter being another three weeks away, there was a notion within the community of men that they could, with some added effort, have the cellar complete before the church holiday.

The suggestion was popular. Within minutes, the men had changed out of their formal worship attire and back into their work clothing, ready to dig. They tapped into a fount of energy they did not know they had.

Though working by lantern light was not ideal and they had to take turns because of the enclosed space in which they were working, there was something about getting a chore accomplished outside the normal hours of their strict schedule that invigorated their work. While one team would go to work with shovels and pickaxes, trying to outdo one another with the chunks of soil they broke off, the other team stood and watched, gulping down mugs of cool water.

They had a straightforward strategy: rather than remove layer by layer by layer of soil from the surface, they had agreed it would be easier to excavate a cave of sorts a couple of feet below the surface of the soil. Having done so, the men would then knock the remaining overhang down into the cavity they had created. It seemed reasonable to everyone involved that if they could get gravity to pull down a ledge of soil two to three feet deep, it was preferable to doing it with manpower. That, therefore, was the tactic they employed.

By midnight, the men of the house had found their rhythm, and even in the dimness of the candlelight, they could see that progress was being made. The more progress the men could see, the more enthusiasm they garnered for the task at hand. Andreas Kresmer was no exception, but unfortunately, his enthusiasm would seal his fate.

The Single Brothers' House as it appeared through the trees of Salem's town square circa 1890. *Collection of Old Salem Museums and Gardens.*

Kresmer, it so happened, was small in stature. Unlike some of the other men who could use their height and arm span to generate momentum on a pickaxe, Kresmer had no choice but to work close to the soil and hope that his work ethic would allow him to keep up with his fellow housemates.

When it was his team's turn to resume digging, he found that he was more efficient at scooping away the heavy dirt if he worked on his knees rather than up on his feet. Kresmer had been trained as a shoemaker, and he was accustomed to crouching over his work. That same hunching posture, he discovered, lent itself well to stabbing his spade into a girth of soil and dragging it away from the mound they were attempting to dispel.

One of the men supervising the job, though, noticed Kresmer on his knees and cautioned him, "Brother Kresmer, I don't think it's wise to work like that. That ledge could give way at any minute."

Just moments later, one of the other men began shouting, "Get back! It's breaking!" The warning, however, came too late for Kresmer. Not heeding the advice of the elder brother, Kresmer had continued to pull at the dirt from his position hunched over on his knees. The suspended overhang of soil collapsed, crushing the shoemaker before he got the opportunity to leap out of the way. Though the other men rushed to excavate their companion from the loosened earth, the trauma was too much for Kresmer, and he died. As the dirt was shoveled off of Kresmer, first his distinctive red cap emerged, and then, below it, his muddied face twisted in agony.

When the cellar was complete, it was a sad reminder to the men in the home of their former housemate. Tragic as the death was, however, the many chores they had to do around the house and the many trades they were variously trying to master served as welcome distractions from the horror of the scene they had witnessed in the cellar.

As the town of Salem evolved, so, too, did the purposing of its buildings. Eventually, the single men who had lived with Kresmer married off and established households of their own or established shops in which to practice their respective trades and moved away from the Single Brothers' House to be closer to their businesses. The so-called Single Brothers' House would ultimately come to lodge a number of older women.

One such woman was the grandmother of Betsy, one of the town's many little girls. Salem is not a large town, and it was not unusual for Betsy to make her way through the town square across from the Single Brothers' House and pay her grandmother a visit. Her grandmother, of course, loved seeing her granddaughter and never refused a visit—until, that is, she heard

A picture from within the cellar Andreas Kresmer died helping to excavate. *Collection of Old Salem Museums and Gardens*.

The Salem Tavern and some of its guests in a photograph from 1882. *Collection of Old Salem Museums and Gardens*.

that someone, or something, in the Single Brothers' House was pursuing her young granddaughter.

Betsy arrived one day at her grandmother's door more excited than usual. The grandmother could sense a different energy about Betsy that day, like something exciting had just happened to the little girl. Yet before her grandmother could inquire, Betsy shared her unique experience with the older woman, saying, "There's a little man out there, and he did this." With that, Betsy pointed at her grandmother, turned her pointed hand over and curled and recurled her index finger into a *C*, beckoning her grandmother to come toward her.

Inexplicable sightings of a "little man" inside the Single Brothers' House did not end there; they grew more specific. Other residents of the house not only started catching glimpses of a short man moving through the hallways of the home, but they also noticed that the man they glimpsed wore a red cap. In due time, Betsy's "little man" came to be known as the "Little Red Man."

In spite of the sightings and the inevitable connection community members started making between Kresmer and the red-capped apparition, the cellar in which Kresmer had died stayed in use. Thus, no one thought twice when one of the town's prominent citizens requested to let one of his guests take a look at the marvel of Moravian engineering, one of countless many throughout the town.

Receiving permission for the request, the community leader, with guest in tow, led the way down the stone steps into the bowels of the Single Brothers' House. Though it was the middle of the day, the light in the cellar was dim and the two men paused a moment at the bottom of the steps to let their eyes adjust. As their pupils widened and the basement's interior became clearer, the men, at the same moment, both laid eyes on the Little Red Man.

Both men felt more challenged by the apparition than they did fazed. Acting on impulse, one of the men leapt at the specter, convinced, somehow, that the spirit could be captured. Emboldened by his counterpart, the other man then lunged for the apparition. Yet there was nothing for the men to grasp; upon making their attempts at tackling the ghost, they found themselves hugging themselves, clutching nothing more than the air between their arms and their torsos. Glancing up at each other and then around the room, they saw the Little Red Man again, but this time he stood grinning as he looked on from a doorway, amused by their foolish attempts to apprehend him.

What about those who still seek a chance encounter with the Little Red Man? For a two-week period each year, the cellar in which Andreas Kresmer

Right: The stone steps that lead down into the cellar in which the Little Red Man has appeared. *Courtesy of Forsyth County Public Library Photograph Collection.*

Below: The Single Brothers' House in which Andreas Kresmer met his tragic end still looms at the corner of Academy Street and Main Street. *Photograph by G.T. Montgomery.*

met his tragic end is, in fact, open to the public for an event called Candle Tea. The event, a Christmas tradition that takes place each December, is a combination of several things including Christmas carols, candle making and Moravian sugar cake. Part of the tradition calls for assembling a small-scale replica (referred to as a *putz*) of Old Salem circa 1900. Not only does the *putz* include nearly one hundred replicas of buildings from within the town, but the entire thing is then covered with white marble dust, which is sprinkled evenly across the scene to create the illusion of a fresh snowfall. It is, without question, an amazing work of art, but look across the table on which it sits, and you might just see the Little Red Man grinning out at you from the shadows.

CHAPTER 7
MARY'S STARE

S traight across Salem's town square, facing the dual front doors of the Single Brothers' House, is the front entrance of Salem College, which was established in 1772 to serve as a school for the young women of the greater Salem area.

One of Salem College's many buildings is an inconspicuous residence hall known on campus simply as Babcock Hall. Nonetheless, though the building may appear benign from the outside, the students who have lived there may tell you the story of the unnerving portrait that stands guard over its lobby.

Mary Reynolds Babcock was the daughter of Richard J. Reynolds, founder of R.J. Reynolds Tobacco Company and creator of Camel cigarettes, and Katherine Reynolds. She was one of four children, having one sister, Nancy Reynolds, and two brothers, Richard Reynolds Jr. and Smith Reynolds. Mary was the second child born to R.J. and Katherine, as well as their first daughter, and as an older sibling, she likely felt some responsibility for her two younger ones. Mary's father died when she was only ten, and her mother passed away when she was sixteen. As for her youngest sibling, Smith, he was only thirteen at the time he lost his second parent, and one could argue that it made way for a handful of wild, hard-partying years before his untimely death at the age of twenty-one.

After the death of the Reynolds parents, care for the children was overtaken by their uncle and aunt, William and Kate Reynolds, but the two guardians could not convince Smith to stay in school. Rather, the young heir decided to quit school and pursue aviation. He considered flying his biggest passion.

Two little girls shown strolling past the Mary Reynolds Babcock Residence Hall in 1957. *Courtesy of Forsyth County Public Library Photograph Collection.*

When he turned eighteen, Smith decided to marry Anne Cannon. The young couple did have a child together but, all the same, got divorced after only two years of marriage. Just days later, Smith married his second wife, Libby Holman, an actress and singer. By 1932, Reynolds and Holman had moved onto his family's estate in Winston-Salem, the so-called Reynolda House, where the two came to be known for their extravagant, over-the-top parties.

One such party, however, would prove to end in mystery and tragedy. As always, Smith and his celebrity wife had no trouble getting guests together for the event. In addition to the lure of their buoyant personalities, the Reynoldses' mansion itself was a magnet for partygoers. The home and grounds left no shortage of entertainment options for guests who made the effort to attend. The estate featured a bowling alley, skating rink and both an indoor and outdoor swimming pool. It also had a custom-made bar area complete with cushioned booths and mirrored backdrops, a picture made complete by Reynolds and Holman's flapper friends twirling long strings of pearls around ring-adorned fingers. When R.J. and Katherine Reynolds finished construction on the mansion in 1917, little did they know that the shooting gallery they also included in its design would prefigure a different shooting in their home: the alleged murder of their youngest son.

Wednesday, July 6, 1932, was just under way. It was a little after 1:00 a.m. Reynolds and Holman's party, though a great fête, had peaked, and a number of guests had left for home. Even Smith and his wife had disappeared into one of the many rooms on the second floor by that time.

Then, like the snap of a bone, a crack rang out through the interior of the mansion. Holman ran to the second-floor balcony and screamed, "Smith's shot himself!" Hearing Holman's hysterical cry, Ab Walker, Reynolds's childhood friend, dashed upstairs, where he found Reynolds sprawled across a bed with blood oozing from a gunshot wound to the side of his head.

With Reynolds still alive somehow, Walker saw to it that he was rushed to the hospital for medical attention. In spite of their efforts to save the youngest offspring of Winston-Salem's most renowned citizen, Smith Reynolds was dead before the sun got the chance to rise.

Reynolds's death was—at first—ruled a suicide, but on further investigation, Winston-Salem's authorities chose to charge both Holman and Walker in connection with the shooting of the Reynolds heir. The Reynolds family, hoping to suppress the scandal around the senseless death, moved for the charges to be dropped, and both Holman and Walker went free. Though the two managed to avoid prison, things would still not end well for them.

Walker, born in 1909, died at only forty-two, four months shy of his forty-third birthday. As for Holman, she relocated from North Carolina after the suspicious death of her husband and eventually settled at a new estate called Treetops in Greenwich, Connecticut. In 1971, however, Holman's mental

An aerial view of God's Acre from 1950. On the horizon, the 1929 tower at the R. J. Reynolds Tobacco Company headquarters can be seen. *Courtesy of Forsyth County Public Library Photograph Collection.*

health took a turn for the worse. In June of that year, Holman went out to her garage, started the ignition of her Rolls-Royce and killed herself.

Completing the sad pattern of tragedy, Reynolds and Holman's only child together, Christopher Reynolds, also met an untimely end, though his birth was a miracle in and of itself. Holman, in fact, was pregnant with her son at the time Smith Reynolds mysteriously died. Some accounts argue that Holman and Reynolds were fighting about the coming child just before the gunshot sounded. Also, when questioned over the shooting, Holman told authorities that, in spite of being pregnant, she had been drinking to the point of blackout.

Still, the pregnancy survived the traumatic events, and—though it happened three months prematurely—Holman gave birth to Christopher on January 10, 1933. Nevertheless, Christopher, or "Topper" as he would come to be known, never made it past his teenaged years. At only seventeen, Reynolds and Holman's one child died in a mountain-climbing accident on California's Mount Whitney.

The great quantity of tragedy and grief within the lives of Mary Reynolds's brother, sister-in-law and nephew is an important factor to weigh when considering the tale of Babcock Hall. The residence hall is, in fact, named for Mary Reynolds, who married Charles Babcock in 1929, thus assuming his last name. Mary was herself a graduate from Salem, from whence she traveled to Paris and studied art for a number of months.

In addition to attaching her name to its newest residence hall, Salem College wanted to honor the Reynolds daughter in another way, too. A portrait of Mary was commissioned, painted and hung in the building's lobby. Portrait in place, the new residence hall opened in 1955, two years after Mary's passing.

That fall semester in 1955, Babcock Hall saw its first residents, who, for the most part, were pleased with their lodging. The building was a great complement to the rest of the architecture on Salem's campus, its beds were as comfortable as to be expected and certain special touches had been provided, such as the pianos in common areas that students could play to unwind. It was a fine housing assignment to receive, all except for one thing: the portrait of Mary Reynolds Babcock hanging in the lobby.

Within the first few weeks of the semester, the female students began to notice something strange about the portrait: no matter where one stood within the foyer of the building, it appeared that the eyes of Mary Reynolds Babcock were locked on your person. Having noticed it but unfazed by the observation, the students went about their way, only mentioning it to one another casually to see if anyone else had noticed the strange nature of the painting. Without fail, most every young lady assigned to live within the residence hall had had the same experience: glancing up in the direction of the piece of art only to find Mary's stare looking back.

As the first few weeks of the semester turned into the first couple of months of the school year, the residents of the building began to test the portrait. Five of them, for example, would scatter themselves about the lobby of the residence hall and all look at the painting simultaneously. Mary, though, found a way to have her gaze locked on each and every student regardless of how many of them stood in the lobby. Even attempts to glance at the painting from the corner of one's eye were met with the steady, unblinking stare of Mary. The students' observations of the portrait, however, would grow stranger yet.

Above: The interior of Salem College's Babcock Hall as seen in a picture from 1957. *Courtesy of Forsyth County Public Library Photograph Collection.*

Left: A photograph from 1962 shows artist Joseph Wallace King, also known as Vinciata, posing beside his completed portrait of Mary Reynolds Babcock. *Courtesy of Forsyth County Public Library Photograph Collection.*

As the novelty of the painting's gaze failed to wear off, it also began to resonate with the students of the residence hall more and more. The stare was so direct and so steady that one could feel it regardless of where one directed one's eyes. Some of the students began to avoid making eye contact with Mary but found they could not escape her gaze. The unnerving quality of the stare prompted a new approach: the residents of the building began greeting the painting when entering the building and bidding it adieu when exiting the building. Somehow offering the humblest "Hi, Mary" or "Bye, Mary" seemed to lessen the immediate effect of the painting's gaze. It was not that the young ladies of Babcock Hall stopped noticing the stare, but something about the exchange of hellos and farewells seemed to make the stare less unsettling.

Of course, not all of the ladies occupying the building subscribed to the notion. Though the tradition quickly became popular with most of the students there, a select few refused to join in the exchange of words with the silent portrait. Little did they know the decision would have consequences.

It took a while for the pattern to emerge, but certain things began happening to those young ladies who refused to acknowledge Mary on their way in and out of Babcock Hall. They were nothing monumental, but the incidents were enough to make life inconvenient. They would show up for a quiz on one chapter only to find they had studied a completely different chapter by mistake and fail the quiz. At times, young ladies found themselves rooting through their backpacks in class trying to find this or that assignment that they swore they had put in their bags before leaving, only to find it later sitting atop their desks or beds back at their rooms. Mary, it appeared, was punishing those young students who refused to give her the most simple of acknowledgements.

By the start of the spring semester in 1956, every young lady living in the residence hall had made it a habit to either greet or say farewell to the painting of Mary in the lobby of their building. To do otherwise was to ask for punishment to come your way. Years on, the necessity of the habit continues to be common knowledge among Salem students, and the never-ending dialogue of "Hi, Mary" and "Bye, Mary" proceeds in the lobby of Babcock Hall.

One cannot help but wonder what instigated Mary's wrathful watch on the students' comings and goings at Babcock Hall, until, that is, one considers the tragedy Mary had to witness in the lives of her younger brother, sister-in-law and teenaged nephew. With that, the painting's ever-watching stare begins to make sense.

By hanging her portrait in such a conspicuous spot where she could watch over young people, Salem College granted to Mary Reynolds Babcock an ongoing chance to keep youths on a path of proper conduct in a way, sadly, she could not with her brother and his family. Thus, for as long as the painting of Mary hangs on the wall of Babcock Hall, she will continue to use her gaze to make the youths within it do good things with their lives.

CHAPTER 8

GRAMLEY'S GHOST

Like Babcock Hall, Salem College's Dale H. Gramley Residence Hall is also not old in comparison to the rest of Old Salem: it was built in 1965. It does have something else in common with Babcock Hall, however: its own strange tale. While the spirit of Mary Babcock keeps Salem's students on the straight and narrow, so to speak, it is hard to say toward what end the ghost of Gramley Hall strives.

Shortly after Gramley Hall opened on campus, a young lady named Margaret enrolled at Salem College. Yet, from the beginning, things did not go well for Margaret. She missed her family that she had left behind in a small town in central North Carolina. The academic workload of college overwhelmed her, and she could not keep up with the interminable reading and writing assignments from her professors. Making matters worse, Margaret struggled to make any close friends. While her fellow classmates were nice and outgoing, Margaret had trouble connecting with them and kept to herself.

Margaret sank into depression. As she tried to stick to her daily routine and hope her spirits would rise, she just fell deeper into despair. When she looked around campus, it seemed like all the other girls had specific groups into which they fit. When she was in class, all the other students appeared to have a better grasp on the material than she did. On her hall, it felt as if every other girl had found that one mate who could be counted on as a best friend, while Margaret just felt alone.

If she had owned a car, she would have just driven home and at the very least spent the weekend with her family, but she did not. She knew that if she

An aerial view of Old Salem as it appeared in 1964. *Collection of Old Salem Museums and Gardens.*

wanted to see her family, she would have to call her father and mother and ask one of them to make the drive up to Winston-Salem to pay her a visit. She also knew she did not have the resolve to do that.

Instead of wanting to call home more often, as one might expect, Margaret found that when she called home she felt immense internal pressure to put on a "happy face" so as to make her parents think that her experience as a college student was going great. They had, after all, worked hard from the day she was born to provide for her, and sending her to Salem was the pinnacle of that effort. They believed that if Margaret could earn a degree from Salem, the number of doors open to her for the rest of her life would be countless. They knew, of course, that James K. Polk's wife was an alumna of the school, but beyond that, they were also aware that several much more recent graduates from the college had gone on to be success stories in their chosen industries. Margaret felt that if she broke down in tears over the phone and told her parents how much she hated the place, not only would she shatter the dream they had for her college education, but by extension she would also shatter their envisioned dream of her future success out in the world.

The tipping point for Margaret came via a failed test. The professor who had administered the exam had not intended to make the exam extra difficult, and it was not as though she had graded Margaret's exam harder than the others. Rather, Margaret accepted, she simply had not mastered the material, and there was no way of hiding it on the exam. Though she had read her assignments, attended class and studied for the exam, when she found herself sitting in the classroom with the blank exam questions staring up at her from the page, she did not know where to begin.

It was not just the fact she failed the exam; moreover, it was the fact that the exam was weighted such that Margaret knew she could not bounce back from the *F* with the time remaining in the semester. What she could not tell her parents about her college experience, Margaret realized, was going to reveal itself when they received her report card. The thought of her parents seeing her failure in black and white on the report card deflated her. She wondered how she could explain to them the true nature of her time away from home as the slow one in class with no friends, no group and, generally, nowhere to belong.

A photograph shows Salem Academy looming through the trees. *Photograph by G.T. Montgomery.*

What went through Margaret's head at the very end will never be known. The evening of the same day in which she received the failed exam back from her professor, she called home and spoke with both of her parents. Though they could sense a weary tone in their daughter's voice, they equated it with fatigue from all the studying and paper writing that Margaret's renowned school probably demanded of her. In spite of the weariness in her voice, Margaret still seemed pleased to speak with them, if, perhaps, a little distant. As always, she was sure to say "I love you" to both of her parents before getting off the line. The last words she heard were from her mother: "I love you, too, darling. Good night."

Margaret then went back to her room, and the waiting began. She waited, first, until her roommate fell asleep. That was not a challenge: her roommate went to bed on the early side, unlike some of the other girls on the hall who were still in and out of the bathroom and common areas up until one and two in the morning. That said, she did not want to run into them either, and thus, she kept waiting.

When she and her roommate first turned off the light in their room, Margaret felt as wide-awake as ever. Her mind felt more alert than normal, and she could feel the pulse of her blood as her heart beat at an elevated rate. Yet as she lay in bed—so as to give her roommate the impression that she, too, was retiring for the night—and waited for everyone else on the hall to fall asleep, she herself dozed. In the course of doing so, she had strange, vivid dreams, and each one woke her with a start, until, at last, she saw that it was just after 3:00 a.m. She knew it was time to proceed with her plan.

She let herself out of her dorm room as quietly as possible and made her way for the steps at the end of her hall. She climbed the steps to the third floor, where she knew no one would bother her. There, pushed up against a wall, Margaret located a large storage crate she had previously scouted in the attic space. She wrapped both hands around the crate's wooden edge and, grunting, dragged it out into the middle of the room. She climbed atop it and then—using the strap she had pilfered from her roommate's bathrobe—hung herself from a rafter.

Like David in the sledding accident on the Bank Street hill, it stands to reason that when a young person dies in this world, the world, sometimes, is not ready to let go. Margaret may be just such a case. Though Margaret had felt she could not carry on any further, the strange happenings on the third floor of Gramley Hall seem to suggest a carrying on from the other side.

Gramley Hall still serves as lodging for Salem College's new generations of students. Though the young ladies assigned to Gramley do not have to greet

The backside of Gramley Hall and Salem College's hillside campus. *Photograph by G.T. Montgomery*.

Looking past the tombstones of Salem Cemetery, one can see the historic buildings of Old Salem in the background. *Photograph by G.T. Montgomery*.

a portrait on their way to and from the building, year in and year out, they do have some unexplainable experiences of their own. Such experiences are especially prevalent with those students given a room on the second floor, for there, below the attic where Margaret took her life, one can hear the spirit of the young suicide victim continue to occupy Gramley Hall's topmost level.

Margaret's spirit expresses itself in a variety of ways, but an especially eerie experience seems common. Just as one of the many second-floor residents is about to fall asleep, the sound of marbles hitting the floor above clatters down from the ceiling. Eerier still, one can hear the marbles roll across the floor until they are brought to a stop.

In other instances, students have heard inexplicable knocking. Without reasonable explanation, the sound of knuckles rapping on a wooden door or plaster wall can be heard. Is Margaret, perhaps, banging on the wooden rafters in an attempt to find a sturdy one?

The most frightening experience of all, though, is the sound of Margaret's spirit reenacting the horrific conclusion to her life. Sometimes in the middle of the night—when total darkness envelopes Old Salem and Gramley Hall—a student will find herself lying awake and fretting over a big paper or exam. It is then that she will hear the dreadful sound of a heavy crate being dragged across the floor above and Margaret, feeling now not her own anxiety but that of each new class's students, taking her life all over again.

CHAPTER 9
STAUB'S SPIRIT

When one walks out of Gramley Hall onto Church Street, one finds him or herself standing at the corner of Church and Blum. Take a quick stroll one block west, and one will find a navy blue sign hanging from a timber that reads "TAVERN—SALEM, NC." Between the two phrases appears a stylized Moravian star of gold, orange and red, inspired, perhaps, by the breathtaking colors of the fall foliage that appear each autumn within the historic district. On either side of the sign jut out black iron poles attached to metal canisters—torches used to illuminate the sign for those travelers making their way into the town after sunset.

The blue sign, however, marks not the original Salem Tavern but instead the so-called Salem Tavern Annex, a wooden structure built in 1816 to supplement the demand of the original tavern building, which is directly south of the annex. Though two distinct buildings now, for a period beginning in 1832, the original tavern and its annex, in another display of Moravian engineering, were connected with a structure built between the two. No less, when pursuing Salem's spirits, one should venture to the southerly building, the brick structure that predates the annex and once served as Old Salem's premier lodging for travelers.

Now known as the Salem Tavern Museum, the brick building that sits next to the yellow-painted, wood-sided tavern annex was built in 1784. The Salem Tavern was built by the town's Moravian settlers as a place to offer food and lodging to visitors passing through the settlement. Such

The Salem Tavern Annex that was built in 1816 to help accommodate Salem's many visitors. *Photograph by G.T. Montgomery.*

an establishment was an important commodity to provide for potential customers patronizing the Moravians' shops and purchasing their goods.

The 1784 version of the tavern, however, was actually a reconstruction built to replace an earlier tavern at the same site. The original tavern was built in 1775, but it, having been constructed of wood, caught fire and burned to the ground. Though the town's leaders were keen enough to use a brick construction when the structure had to be built a second time, they could not have predicted that one of its future guests would put even the strength of the brick to the test when setting off a bomb of sorts in the room in which he was boarding.

Augustus Staub was renting one of the second-floor rooms in the Salem Tavern. He did not need anything spacious in that he was staying there by himself, but he did make it clear that he valued his privacy. He did not encourage the staff of the tavern to check in on his room but, rather, preferred to watch over his things himself and initiate any services by the tavern staff via direct request from him to them.

What the tavern staff may not have realized was the fact that Staub was using the room as his personal chemistry laboratory. Various reports do not conclude why Staub was practicing chemistry and what end he may have been trying to reach, but one thing history makes clear is the fact that Staub was transporting various chemicals into the tavern and using the privacy of his room to mix them with one another. Unfortunately for Staub, on the night of Sunday, August 2, 1857, he mixed the wrong two components together.

Between 11:30 p.m. and midnight, Salem Tavern was rocked by a blast. Whichever chemicals Staub had combined exploded on contact and set the walls of the Salem Tavern afire. Throughout the streets of Salem, the clang of fire bells sounded in the darkness of the night, and the men of the town assembled to fight the fire now blazing at the inn. Staub had, somehow, survived the explosion, but his body was covered from head to toe with severe burns. In the end, the injuries proved too much. Within a matter of hours, the amateur chemist was dead.

After the explosion the building incurred, the proprietor of the inn, Adam Butner, was awarded $200 from the estate of Staub to help defray the expense of repairing the damaged lodge. Additionally, Old Salem Museums and Gardens restored the structure in 1965, and at a glance, there is no remnant of the detonation that killed Staub and ruined part of the building. Though no longer open to boarders, the structure is open to visitors. Today, the tavern serves as one of Old Salem Museums and Gardens' premier exhibits.

Above: The Salem Tavern as it appears today. *Photograph by G.T. Montgomery.*

Left: Look long enough, and you might see the spirit of August Staub rustling the curtains of his room in the Salem Tavern. *Photograph by G.T. Montgomery.*

Yet, for an experience outside the normal OSMG tour, one might consider walking past the eighteenth-century tavern just before midnight one evening. By then, the building, of course, should be empty: no interpreters, no tourists, no custodians. Look up at the windows of the second story, though, and see if you cannot spot some curtains being pulled to the side. For though the Salem Tavern has been closed to boarders for decades, some say the spirit of Augustus Staub still resides in the very room in which, either by intention or accident, he took his own life. Might he still look out from the window and rue forevermore his poorly planned chemistry experiment?

CHAPTER 10

SPECTER IN THE SALEM TAVERN

Before its near calamity at the hands of Augustus Staub, the Salem Tavern was open for business when a stranger to the town arrived at the inn on horseback seeking a place to stay. The man, of course, was offered a room, but it became immediately evident that the visitor also needed medical attention. The tavern keeper who checked in the man could see the traveler was very sick and called for a doctor to tend to the tavern guest. Nevertheless, in spite of the doctor's efforts, the guest slipped into a coma. Shortly thereafter, the man died.

Unfortunately, the combination of the man's grave illness and the tavern keeper's scramble to secure medical care meant no identifying information about the traveler was determined prior to his death. Upon his passing, the town's authorities did a thorough search through his saddlebags and examined his clothing, but nothing about the two provided any information about the man's identity or place of origin. Having no way either to determine the gentleman's particulars or contact his next of kin, the Moravians interred the man in the so-called "Strangers' Graveyard," the cemetery in which they laid to rest all non-Moravian strangers to the town.

In the town of Salem, such was the custom that the Salem Moravian Graveyard was only used for the burial of Moravian members of European heritage in the congregation. Practicing Moravians of African heritage were laid to rest in a different cemetery at the southern end of Salem, now called, fittingly, the "African-American Graveyard."

An unidentifiable grave in the Strangers' Graveyard is marked simply as "ADULT."
Photograph by G.T. Montgomery.

Non-Moravians, however, who passed away while visiting Salem were interred in yet a third cemetery—the so-called Strangers' Graveyard. The Strangers' Graveyard, sometimes also referred to as the "Parish Graveyard," was used for forty years from the period of 1775 through 1815. Though the town's leaders thought the Strangers' Graveyard to be the best resting place for the tavern's expired, anonymous boarder, they would soon find out it would be an uneasy rest.

In the days following the man's death, the servants in the tavern began to have strange experiences. The workers heard unusual noises that seemed to have no cause or explanation. They also reported feeling "cold spots"—distinct instances where the air in one of the tavern's rooms would turn icy and send chills through the servants. Both of these occurrences, the servants claimed, only started after the nameless visitor expired. To the dismay of the tavern keeper, the workers became convinced that a ghost was haunting the Salem Tavern. The servants grew so increasingly frightened of encountering the spirit that they even refused to go in the building's basement unaccompanied by a fellow co-worker. Soon even the tavern's skeptical innkeeper would not be able to deny the restless soul's presence in the lodging.

One night, with the interior of the tavern lit only by flickering candlelight, the tavern keeper was in his office working. In an instant, the door to the office flew open, and one of the tavern's maids, hysterical with fright, rushed into the keeper's study. All color had drained from her face, and she exclaimed to the tavern keeper that just moments before, she had experienced the building's wandering spirit. At that moment, the maid's manager knew he needed to confront the ghost rumors once and for all. He shoved back his chair from his desk, picked up a lantern and strode out into the shadowy hallway. What happened next would become an essential episode in Salem's canon of spiritual sightings.

The tavern keeper walked across the floor's wooden planks and peered through the yellow glow of candlelight. Undeniably, a human-like figure appeared in front of him. As the keeper stood there face to face (as it were) with the ghostly apparition, the spirit spoke, saying something akin to: "I am the man you buried. My brother is in Texas. Please tell him I am dead." The spirit then told the tavern keeper his name. With that, the haunt vanished, and the stunned manager of the tavern was left standing alone in an empty corridor.

Immediately, using the information the ghost had provided, the tavern keeper began composing a letter to the man in Texas alleged to be the dead man's brother. As requested, the keeper mentioned the deceased man by the name he had been told and explained the circumstances of the traveler's death. The letter was sent on its long journey west, and the manager of the lodge had no choice but to wait to see what would happen.

As miraculous as it was mysterious, the tavern keeper was sent a reply. The gentleman in Texas who had received the letter from Salem did, supposedly, have a brother who had traveled to North Carolina, from whom he had not heard since and of whose whereabouts he had no idea. Nonetheless, the brother in Texas did not, in fact, travel to Salem to recover his sibling's already-interred body, nor did he question the way in which the Moravians had treated his brother when he fell ill, but he did make one request. He asked that his fallen brother's belongings be sent to him in Texas. The tavern's keeper—eager, of course, to eliminate any reason for the spirit to linger—gladly obliged and had his brief guest's clothes and saddlebags sent west. After doing so, the tavern keeper never again beheld the apparition.

Many questions, obviously, remain. For one, was the recipient of the letter sent to Texas indeed the anonymous lodger's brother, or just someone who saw an opportunity to act the part and, in turn, collect on some unclaimed

Might the footfalls atop their graves awaken the spirits of the residents in the Strangers' Graveyard? *Photograph by G.T. Montgomery.*

A gnarled tree marks the southeast corner of Salem Cemetery. *Photograph by G.T. Montgomery.*

possessions? If that were the case, however, why would that have appeased the restless soul haunting the tavern?

With regard to the tavern's ghost, was his primary objective to communicate to his family his ultimate fate and save them from a lifetime of wondering? Or, perhaps, did the spirit want his brother notified because there was something hidden in his saddlebags that he did not want falling into just any person's hands? One wonders what that something might have been. For the brother in Texas to specifically request that his sibling's left-behind possessions be sent halfway across the country by horseback does make one curious about the contents of those saddlebags. If the dead man's belongings were a factor in the tavern's haunting, one presumes they were sent to the right person, or the restless soul would not have been satisfied.

If, however, they were sent to an impostor in Texas, is it possible the tavern ghost still wanders Old Salem, passing between the historic buildings while waiting for his possessions to finally, rightfully make their way back to one of his descendants? Fortunately for present-day ghost hunters, it is easy enough to visit the historic district and hope that one might catch a glimpse of the traveler's spirit.

PART III
ADDENDUM

CHAPTER 11

ANOTHER MYSTERIOUS SHOOTING

If you found the mystery of Smith Reynolds's death intriguing in "Mary's Stare," you may also be interested in this story of yet another notorious Winston-Salem shooting. Though it does not take place on the grounds of Old Salem nor involve a ghost per se, it is a chilling tale all the same.

Does the name "Mary Ellen Smith" sound familiar? One may recognize the latter half of the name from the oft-covered bluegrass song "Poor Ellen Smith." What many do not realize is that poor Ellen Smith was very much a real person and that the murder that inspired a song took place in the heart of Winston-Salem, North Carolina.

On Tuesday, July 19, 1892, Ellen Smith received a note from her former suitor, Peter DeGraff. Smith and DeGraff had started dating soon after meeting in January 1890, and Smith became pregnant in 1891, accusing DeGraff of being the child's father. The child passed away either at birth or soon thereafter, and the relationship soured. The couple remained broken up—until, that is, Smith received DeGraff's note on that fateful Tuesday in July 1892. It would prove to be her second-to-last day seen alive.

According to reports from the time, the note Smith received was conciliatory in nature. DeGraff's correspondence communicated to Smith that he was still in love with her and wanted to meet with her in person. DeGraff requested that Smith meet him the next day—Wednesday, July 20, 1892—by a spring (a tributary, perhaps, that fed into Peters Creek that runs through present-day Hanes Park) adjacent to the luxurious Hotel

Zinzendorf. One can imagine Smith's excitement—not only did her former lover seemingly want to reconcile, but he also wanted to do so in a romantic setting by the city's most elegant inn. In reality, the secluded nature of the couple's meeting place would prove fatal to Ellen Smith. There, on the morning of July 21, she was found dead.

The last time Smith was seen alive was on the afternoon of July 20. Before boarding a streetcar bound for the Hotel Zinzendorf, the young lady stopped at the Coles & Rose Store to purchase a yellow handkerchief, the final accessory, presumably, to the outfit she had chosen to impress Peter DeGraff that day. Nevertheless, on the morning of the next day, the Hotel Zinzendorf's laundry attendant, Harriet Pratt, encountered a man who told her (as recorded by Jennifer Bean Bower), "a woman was lying dead in the woods and insisted that she go and look." The woman was Ellen Smith. An autopsy performed soon thereafter determined she had died from a single gunshot wound through her heart—a gruesome twist in the murder of one who'd hoped to have her heart unbroken. During the examination of Smith's body, DeGraff's note from July 19 was also found—it was tucked close to Smith's bosom where she had, one can speculate, put it for safekeeping.

DeGraff immediately became the prime suspect in Smith's murder, but he was able to flee town before being arrested. The accused man did not travel far, however. Documents show DeGraff fled to Mount Airy, North Carolina, a town about forty miles north of Winston-Salem. In Mount Airy, DeGraff took on the name of either H.C. Hendricks or H.D. Hendricks and worked for almost a year at Yokely's Sawmill. Then, on June 22, 1893, DeGraff made the fateful decision to return to the town of Winston, North Carolina, but this time he would not avoid capture.

On the very day Peter DeGraff reentered the city limits of Winston, a passerby recognized the wanted man and notified Forsyth County sheriff R.M. McArthur. By that evening, McArthur had DeGraff in custody, and the process of prosecuting the fugitive went into effect. DeGraff's trial for murder began on Friday, August 11, 1893. A variety of witnesses were called by the prosecution and the defense, but particularly incriminating was the testimony of D.H. Hudson, who (as also reported by Jennifer Bean Bower) testified to the court "that DeGraff claimed Ellen had cheated on him, and then threatened to 'shoot her heart out.'" Nonetheless, DeGraff did take to the stand in his own defense, claiming he had seen Smith at the spring the day of her murder but that he had seen her with another man, who, upon spotting DeGraff, had started shooting at him. Though DeGraff tried to shift blame to that armed, unidentified man, on August 15, just four days after the murder trial had begun, the selected jury found DeGraff guilty of murder. That same morning, the presiding judge, Robert W. Winston, sentenced DeGraff to be executed by hanging.

On the date of DeGraff's execution, February 8, 1894, some accounts estimate as many as six thousand people gathered to watch the convict put to death. Though nothing currently marks the spot, records from the time indicate the site of the gallows was selected to be about three miles north of Winston proper at a site on Liberty Street. If one drives three miles north of downtown Winston-Salem on Liberty Street now, one finds only a scattering of businesses and the northwestern edge of Piedmont Park. That area proved to bear witness to the last public execution in Winston-Salem. The meting out of DeGraff's punishment drew such a crowd and such attention that city leaders subsequently decided future executions would take place out of the public eye.

At 11:00 a.m. on February 8, DeGraff was led from his jail cell at the Forsyth County Jail to the gallows. His death warrant was read aloud, a sermon was given and a prayer was said on DeGraff's behalf. Peter DeGraff then had one last chance to address the crowd, at which point the convicted man had a sudden change of heart. In his final words, DeGraff confessed. According to an 1894 newspaper article documenting the event, DeGraff stated, "I put the pistol to her side and fired. She said but one word...'Lord, have mercy upon me!'" By way of explanation DeGraff also shared with the gathered crowd, "Corn liquor, card playing, dice, pistols and bad women have been my ruin...I am going to God." Moments later, the execution was finished.

Though Winston-Salem has no public memorial to Ellen Smith mourning her tragic end, her story is not forgotten. A quick Internet search for the words "poor Ellen Smith" brings to light a number of music videos (from musicians as varied as Jimmy Martin and Neko Case) featuring the ballad that came to commemorate the sad tale. Though many years have passed since Ellen Smith's final visit to that spring in Winston-Salem, with each singing of the song, the memory of the young girl is kept alive.

CHAPTER 12

ANOTHER HOTEL BLAZE

If you found the tavern blaze intriguing in "Staub's Spirit," you may be interested in this story of a separate hotel that Winston-Salem did lose to fire. Though the Hotel Zinzendorf was built outside of the Old Salem historic district, the tale of its destruction is memorable and serves as another intriguing piece of history from the larger Winston-Salem area.

Today, when one stands at the corner of Glade and Fourth Streets in the historic West End of Winston-Salem, one spies the headquarters of Leonard, Ryden and Burr Real Estate Company. That building, however, is a more recent addition to the landscape. Before there were offices there to sell real estate, that corner *was* prime real estate. It was the home of the grand "Hotel Zinzendorf."

The Hotel Zinzendorf—so named in honor of Count Zinzendorf, benefactor to the original Moravians who settled Salem, North Carolina—opened in May 1892 and was impossible to overlook. The lodging was four stories tall, spanned the distance of a football field in length and was accented with a front porch eighteen feet wide. Numerous turrets with pointed cone roofs graced its façade.

The hotel was a wooden structure built employing the "Shingle style," a style choice borrowed from New England, the home of its designers. Though the project of building the monumental Hotel Zinzendorf was undertaken by the West End Hotel and Land Company of the time, the structure itself was actually designed by an architecture firm based in Boston,

Massachusetts—Wheelwright and Haven, the same firm that designed the 1909 Boston Opera House.

When the resort hotel did open, it was a great success. On its list of visitors were Henry Ford, Harvey Firestone and Thomas Edison, who, in fact, was also an investor in the grandiose inn. Throughout the summer and autumn seasons of 1892, the Hotel Zinzendorf was a popular attraction. Sadly, that success would not last long.

On Thanksgiving Day of that same inaugural year, the colossal hotel encountered a threat it would not be able to endure: fire. That fateful Thanksgiving, fire broke out at the lodging, and in just a matter of two hours, the Hotel Zinzendorf completely burned to the ground. The destruction was so thorough that the only vestige of the hotel grounds still left at the site today is a stone stairwell that leads to nothing in particular.

The Hotel Zinzendorf is Winston-Salem's own reminder that even the grandest of human designs are impermanent. Where once stood a magnificent resort, there is a much humbler real estate office and a simple historical marker summarizing the hotel's saga in just a few lines. Even though the Hotel Zinzendorf no longer stands, its story continues to fascinate and remind Winston-Salem residents of their town's rich cultural history.

CHAPTER 13

THE MORAVIAN STAR

If you were curious about the mention of "Moravian star" at the start of "Staub's Spirit," you may be interested in this explanation of the origins of the quintessential Moravian symbol. As you will find, it has a history all its own.

From the first Sunday of Advent until the Feast of the Epiphany on January 6 ("the twelfth day of Christmas"), it is difficult not to notice the ubiquity of a certain, special decoration adorning homes throughout the Winston-Salem area: an illuminated, white, twenty-six-pointed star. As popular a decoration as it still is today, the origin of that star—more precisely known as a "Moravian star"—dates back, in fact, over 150 years to the small town of Niesky in Saxony, Germany. Though incredible to think an adornment from before the Civil War from a town 4,500 miles away with a population of just eleven thousand people is still the enduring symbol of the Christmas season here in Winston-Salem, as with so much in the Twin City, it is—as suggested by its name—directly connected to the Moravians who helped develop the area.

Although Moravian settlers arrived in the Winston-Salem area as early as 1752, the birth of the Moravian star did not occur for another century and—initially—had nothing to do with celebrating Christmas. Rather, starting in about 1850, the star came to be as a result of a geometry lesson given to young German boys in school at the Moravian settlement in Niesky. Interestingly, Benjamin Henry Boneval Latrobe—the gentleman hired by Thomas Jefferson to oversee the construction of the U.S. Capitol building—attended that same Moravian school in Niesky from 1776 to 1782. Latrobe also went on to design the front gate of the Washington, D.C. Navy Yard; assist in the construction of the Baltimore Basilica; and draw up the central tower for the St. Louis Cathedral on Jackson Square in New Orleans.

What was the assignment given to the students at Latrobe's alma mater? Beginning with plain, flat paper, the project was to craft twenty-six star points (eighteen square-based and eight triangle-based) that could be attached centrally to create a three-dimensional star. As class after class of German boys began crafting the stars, the small Moravian-settled town realized what a unique decoration the stars made for celebrating the birth of Christ.

For one thing, the students' stars hearkened back to the narrative of Jesus's birth in the Gospel of Matthew (2:9): "When [the magi] had heard the king, they set out; and there, ahead of them, went the star that they had seen at its rising, until it stopped over the place where The Child was." The paper stars also served as a fitting reference to Jesus's own words at verse 12 of chapter 8 in the Gospel of John: "Again Jesus spoke to them, saying, 'I am the light of the world. Whoever follows me will never walk in darkness, but will have the light of life.'" Of course, the advent of electric lights made the stars an even more telling illustration of Christ "lighting the darkness." Light bulbs were eventually put in the stars to illuminate them from within, and the decoration we know today—lit up and hanging on so many local front porches every December—was born.

The popularity of the star within the Moravian congregation in Niesky migrated with the Moravians themselves. It is no wonder that the two cities in the United States with the highest concentrations of Moravians and deepest roots to the original European branches of the Moravian Church—Winston-Salem and Bethlehem, Pennsylvania—still, without fail, display their Moravian stars each Advent and Christmas season. Whether it is the thirty-one-foot rendition that sits atop the Wake Forest Baptist Medical Center each holiday season or the multitude that light up the covered bridge between Old Salem and its Visitor Center each winter, the Moravian star is a symbol with a long, international history.

AFTERWORD

U ndertaking the writing of *Ghosts of Old Salem* elicited a number of
questions in my mind, but as I write this, one in particular stands out:
why do cemeteries have such a keen ability to stir the imagination? While
working on this project, I spent time in the three cemeteries that surround
Old Salem, and each seemed to touch me in its own way. I want to say it
is something akin to that feeling one has when hearing the opening notes
of Bach's *Toccata and Fugue in D Minor*, but I think that would be to put too
"spooky" a spin on it. At the same time, though it may not be spooky, that
certain quality a graveyard possesses is different from the sound of angels
singing or that note we hear in our head when we see the clouds break open
and sunlight splay out between them. Perhaps that unique quality can only
be equated with the certain quietness graveyards so often have, and that is
why each attempt at ascribing a musical analogy seems inaccurate.

Atop the desk at which I write this, I have a four-by-six color photograph
I took at Winston-Salem's Dixie Classic Fair a few years ago. As my wife and
I walked around the fair, my eye was caught by an attraction done up like a
haunted house. We were already en route to the Ferris wheel and thus did
not stop for the horror-inspired "ride," but I was drawn to the artwork on
the side of the trailer housing the attraction and did take a beat to snap the
shot now sitting on the desk.

A woman in a pink dress (and comically crooked bosom) occupies the
center of the scene, and to her left, some type of blue ghoul or goblin stands
with one of her arms in its clasp. On her right side, another ghoul—this

The hillside graves of Salem Cemetery. *Photograph by G. T. Montgomery.*

one more skeleton-like—appears to be making its way toward her. As if she were not in enough trouble, the tombstone she is standing behind is starting to crumble, and two giant, boney hands, their nails long and yellowed, are shown reaching up through the soil to also grab, one can presume, the damsel in distress. The horror of the moment is so terrifying, the young woman's black hair seems to have developed instant streaks of gray. Yet, in spite of being a wonderful, colorful comic book–like take on the restless coffin, it, too, does not seem to epitomize that feeling the average graveyard can have on a person.

Rather, if I were to try and put it in words, that quality that seems near-universal in the cemeteries through which I have strolled is tranquility. On those occasions (other than funerals, of course) that I find myself in a cemetery, it always seems like some of the most peaceful moments for which a person could ask. I think of the soft grass that grows between the stones, the birds that flit from tree to tree and that one-of-a-kind quietness that seems to be a constant on the grounds.

When I visited the cemeteries of Old Salem to write this book, I did see a lot of "spooky" things—if I wanted to see them that way. I found crooked metal fences marking family plots, gnarled trees that stood out on

The Salem Moravian Graveyard, more commonly known as "God's Acre," as it appears today. *Photograph by G. T. Montgomery.*

the backdrop of ash-gray skies and black ravens foretelling, I suppose, the mortality that awaits us all. I daresay I even experienced a chill or two that made the hair on the back of my neck stand on end.

That said, when I look back on my memories of Salem Cemetery, God's Acre and the Strangers' Graveyard, I think of peaceful places where souls who experienced all the ups and downs that inevitably come with living life have found their rest. May your experience of Old Salem's burial grounds elicit more peace than it does fear, and as I mentioned in my letter at the start of the book, may any soul seeking rest find it.

I appreciate you allowing me the space to let my mind wander, but ultimately, I realize that if you are reading this book, then you probably started it with the fundamental hope of hearing hair-raising ghost stories. With that in mind, I would like to share with you one last tale before the book comes to a close.

However, before I get to the tale itself, I should introduce it thus: one element missing from the stories told previously within these pages was a story of a freestanding haunted house. Of the tales already shared, there were instances of hauntings within a group home, college residence halls and a tavern, but none of the tales took on that particular type of ghost story in which an individual house is taken over by a spirit. That, in large part, motivates me to share the one last yarn below. In the interest of full disclosure, though it is set in the Carolinas, it is not—my apologies—specific to Old Salem. As for its veracity, I will leave that up to the reader to decide.

Night at 44 Georgian

I arrived at 44 Georgian Street a little after nine, and by the time I'd crossed the black backyard from my car to the front door, I was soaked from the driving rain. The light above the door was either burnt out or not on, making fitting the key into either of the door's two locks a chore unto itself. After a few attempts at each though, both bolts sprung back, and the door swung open into the dark house. My weekend retreat was not off to a very welcoming start.

Nevertheless, after turning on some lights, changing into some dry clothes and settling down in front of the television with a beer, I began to feel more relaxed. After half an hour, I remembered why I'd made the trip in the first place, and suddenly a bowl of Kraft Macaroni & Cheese and a can of Budweiser felt like the best vacation in the world. Even the rain, which had seemed like such a nuisance, now seemed pleasant. Echoes of the drops hitting the roof filled the large, empty house with some welcome background noise.

I was depositing my dirty dishes in the sink when I thought I heard something other than the beating of the rain and the voices on the television. It sounded like a toilet had flushed somewhere in the house. I didn't think someone else was in the house—it felt much too empty for that—but I couldn't resist calling out, "Hello?"

"Hello?" I said again, as I walked toward the steep wooden stairs in the middle of the home. "Anybody there?"

I peered up through the levels of the stairwell. No one answered. Just to ease my jumpy mind, however, I started up the creaky steps so as to confirm my solitude.

On the second floor, everything was still except for an alarm clock blinking *12:00, 12:00, 12:00*. I switched on the lights in both the restrooms on the second floor, and nothing seemed out of place. Unable to put my mind at ease though, I gazed up the steps to the third floor. Once again, I said aloud, "Hello?"

The drumming of the rain on the roof was the only response I received. I still wanted to rule out unknown squatters, and thus I climbed the final steps to the top floor. Though not pitch-black, it was dark enough at the top of the stairs to make it difficult to see. Now I could hear something: running water. I fumbled my hand up and down the wall until I found the light switch. I flipped on the galley-style sconces at the top of the landing and walked toward the third-floor bathroom. The sound of the water, it turned out, was from the faucet in the bathroom sink, which was on and running. I turned it off and said to myself, "Well, this month's water bill is going to be a little high."

I wasn't too concerned though. The sink was not overflowing, and I figured the maid service had probably left it running by accident when cleaning after the departure of the last houseguests.

Satisfied that I'd corrected that problem, I remembered the initial reason that I was up there: the sound of the toilet. I lifted the lid on the toilet bowl and could see the water was stirring. I also removed the lid from the tank on the back of the commode. The flapper was not sitting properly in its opening, thus allowing a small stream of water to keep flowing into the bowl.

"That," I thought, "explains the flush I heard." I pushed the black piece of rubber snugly into the hole at the bottom of the tank, switched off the bathroom light and returned down the wooden steps to reassume my position in front of the TV, feet kicked up and beer in hand.

I had not been flipping channels more than ten minutes when I heard the toilet flush again. Grumbling to myself, I re-climbed the plethora of stairs leading to the third floor. At the top of the stairs, the light I had left on was still lit, but when I turned to walk through the bedroom, I was surprised—the light in the bathroom was also burning. I thought I had switched it off after fixing the toilet, but the yellow pyramid of light splayed out from the bathroom door said otherwise. As I crossed the dark bedroom to the washroom, even more surprising to me, however, was the sound of the faucet running yet again.

I stepped into the bathroom, and not only was water flowing from the sink's faucet, but—stranger yet—water was running in the bathtub as well. I shut them both off and cut the water to the toilet, but now I was uncomfortable.

At first, I was willing to accept that the cleaning crew had left the water running or, by some idiosyncrasy of the plumbing, that the flow had somehow started on its own, but I was finding it difficult to believe the same trick of plumbing had also forced on the tub's faucet. Unsure of what to do, I entered the study outside the restroom and listened. All I could hear was the steady beat of the hard rain on the roof. Once more I said, "Hello?"

No reply. Then, in an effort to let any potential squatters know I had temporarily moved into the house and that they would have to move on to new accommodations, I shouted: "HELLO?!"

The emptiness of the three-story house swallowed the sound.

I turned on the light in the study. A quick glance proved no one was hiding there. Next, I turned on the light in the bedroom that attached to the restroom and study. Again, there was nobody to be seen.

From there, it was a check of every room in the house. The bedroom across the hall—no one. Down the steps, onto the landing, into the guest bedroom—nobody. There was a sharp *POP* as I flipped the light switch in the master bathroom. The source of the noise, however, was just an incandescent light bulb above the sink, its filament no longer able to withstand a current.

All the same, the search uncovered no squatters or any other person who might have been using the third-floor restroom. A check under all the beds, behind all the doors and in all the remaining rooms did not turn up any other "guests" at 44 Georgian. Though still uneasy, I was confident in my search. I felt that if someone had been there, he or she must have slipped out downstairs while I searched upstairs. That was fine with me as long as he or she was gone.

I was still a bit on edge but also growing tired. I contemplated calling the police, but waiting for them to arrive and conduct the exact same search I'd just executed seemed exhausting. Instead, I turned off the TV, finished the last of the beer in my open can and mustered the energy to check the lock on every door and window on the ground floor. I even latched close the shutters on the inside of the windows. If someone had been staying rent-free, I certainly didn't want him or her sneaking back in overnight to retrieve a forgotten parcel.

At this point, I had on every light in the house, and when I finished double-checking that the front door was locked, I stared at the light switch next to it for a long moment. I did feel assured I was the only person in the house, but I couldn't seem to shake my unease. Thus, Al Gore be damned, I decided to leave the lights on for the night.

I did want the tranquility of sleeping in the dark, though. Consequently, I flicked off the light fixtures in the master bedroom before getting into bed. Other than that, the house was lit up like a ceramic Christmas decoration.

I set the alarm clock for nine the next morning, and—in spite of the unexplained events in the third-floor bathroom that evening—by midnight, I feel confident saying, I was asleep.

Not for long. At 1:00 a.m. sharp, the alarm clock by my bed started screeching. I jumped awake to the piercing sound of "*EENK, EENK, EENK, EENK*." In the confusion of being half asleep, I fumbled for the off switch on the clock. After pressing every other button, I found the switch for the alarm and slid it to the off position. Though certain I had set the alarm for nine, at that moment I didn't care about the time: I was more surprised to see that every light in my room was on and burning bright.

Over the bed, a chandelier of translucent shells glowed; above the fireplace, two half-globe spotlights lit a painting on the wall; yellow spilled from beneath the shades of the bedside lamps; and, furthermore, every light in the master bathroom had been turned on: in the shower, above the tub and over the toilet. To top it all off, the bulb above the vanity that had popped earlier was now shining as brightly as ever.

I could not believe my eyes. I *knew* I had turned off all those lights before lying down, and now they were *all* switched on and illuminated. As stunned as I was, I was about to be more so: through the transom window above the bedroom door, I could see that all the lights in the hallway had been darkened.

Although I had every reason to believe someone was in the house with me, the home felt empty as could be. Aside from the rain outside still coming down in buckets, nothing moved. I padded across the bedroom, turned the knobs on the French doors leading out into the hallway and slowly pulled them open. I took a step out into the blackness.

Outside of the bedroom, there was only darkness. I realized that just as every light had been turned on in the master bedroom suite, every other light had been turned off in the rest of the house. It was black at the top of the stairs, at the bottom of the stairs and across the remainder of the second floor.

At that moment, lightning lit the interior of the house, and thunder rattled the panes in the windows. With that, *everything* went dark. The few lights that had been left on went dead.

Back in the bedroom, even the alarm clock was no longer glowing. I suddenly got the distinct feeling I wasn't alone. Like a fool, again, as if to receive an answer, I said aloud, "Hello?"

No response. Just the sound of rain in a dark house, and then: *BANG! BANG! BANG!* Someone was knocking on the front door. I paused. Was my mind playing tricks on me? I waited another beat and then heard again: *BANG! BANG! BANG!*, this time more intense than the last.

Not knowing who could be at the front door at 1:00 a.m. in the middle of a power outage, and not knowing what else to do, I stumbled out of the bedroom and into the hallway and started descending the steep wooden steps. Halfway down, I heard the pounding on the door once more: *BANG! BANG! BANG!*, the sound echoing off the hardwood floors throughout the first floor. The urgent knocks sounded like those of someone in trouble, allowing them to overcome my paralysis born from the other events of the evening. I hurried my pace down the stairs and started fumbling with the locks on the door. In the darkness, I struggled to disengage them while the knocking on the door continued, *BANG! BANG! BANG!*

"Just a minute!" I yelled. "I'm coming!" A second later, both locks snapped back, and I grabbed open the door. No one was there. Exasperated, I shouted out into the side yard into which the door opened, turning my head left and then right, "HELLO?! ANYBODY THERE?!"

There was no sign of anyone out in the rain pouring down on the brick walkway. I could even see the gate out to the street was firmly shut. Whoever had been pounding on the door had vanished in the matter of a moment. I looked both ways once more, shut the door and relocked both locks.

Now I was angry. I was tired, the entire house was pitch-black and I didn't know where to begin looking for candles or a flashlight. The unexplained events in the house had played on my nerves to the point that my hands were shaking, and now some punk was pounding on the door only to disappear before I could get it open.

I decided to call the police. Conveniently, the house's phone was just inside the parlor to the right of the front door. I picked up the headset, and its numbers came to life with green light.

"Well, thank goodness something works," I thought and punched *9-1-1*. A click, and then: "If you'd like to make a call, please hang up and try again." Just when I thought things couldn't get worse, even 911 wouldn't work. I slammed the headset back onto its cradle and picked it up again. Things had gotten worse. The green light behind the keys of the phone was now dead, too. I pressed some buttons and held the phone up to my ear, but this time there was no sound—no operator, no dial tone, no static. Just silence. At a loss for what else to try, I gently set the phone back on its cradle and picked it back up with bated breath. Still no light behind the numbers and no sound across the line. Maybe the malfunctioning phone was the result of my aggression having slammed the thing down too hard or a consequence of the ongoing storm outside, but it occurred to me that it might also be the antics of the same person turning on and off the lights. One thing was certain: the phone was dead.

At that instant, my mind flashed back to when I'd packed my bag not even twenty-four hours earlier. One of the last things I had packed was my cell phone and its charger. I could even recall the pocket of my bag where I had deposited them. Yet, I'd had a change of heart.

"This is supposed to be a retreat," I had told myself. "Do you really need to take your cell phone?" I had known there would be a phone with a "landline" in the house, and I'd felt confident any calls to my cell could be returned after my short vacation. Thus, just before I'd zipped my bags close—I recalled as I stood there in the black sitting room of 44 Georgian holding the inoperable phone—I'd plucked out my cell phone and charger and left them at home. I cursed myself for having made the last-minute decision.

I hung up the lifeless phone. The rain was beating harder against the glass of the windows, and its echo in the house was the loudest it had been since I got there. Though desperate to determine what to do next, the chatter of the pelting raindrops made it difficult to hear myself think.

I decided that my top priority was finding the keys to the car. The banging on the door had distracted me, but I remembered the possibility that I was not alone in the house. I knew that if I could get to the keys, I could make a run to the car and drive to a nearby police station.

Unfortunately, I wasn't sure where the keys were. It was possible I had left them in the pocket of the pants I'd worn earlier, but I felt it was also possible I had dropped them on the kitchen counter when I'd first entered the house. Because one required walking back up the stairs, finding the pants and rooting through the pockets, and the other required passing through the dining room and feeling around the countertop, I decided to check the kitchen first.

I made my way across the small foyer separating the sitting room from the dining room. Each two-hundred-year-old piece of wood in the floorboards squeaked at a different pitch as I tried to tiptoe my body toward the kitchen. On the off chance the intruder didn't know where I was in the blackness, I wanted to keep it that way. I reached out and found the doorframe leading into the dining room.

As soon as I stepped into the dining room, I heard something. It was the sound of clothes rustling. It seemed as if the sound had come from just a few yards away. I froze. I looked around the dark room. I could make out the large disc that was the dining table, and some chairs pressed up against the wall, but if someone was in the room with me, I couldn't locate him or her without the help of light. Across the back wall, I could discern the glass-fronted cabinets filled with china and crystal, but the dishes themselves were unrecognizable, just shadows in shadow boxes. I tried to will my ears to listen harder and better, but whatever sound I'd heard did not reoccur. I stood there listening for what felt like ten minutes, and not sensing any movement other than the up and down of my breathing and the precipitation falling outside, I decided to continue to the kitchen.

Arms outstretched, I found the edge of the countertop. I slid my hands over the surface feeling for my keys. There was an empty glass, the box from the earlier mac 'n' cheese and an unopened bag of sunflower seeds I'd brought, but, alas, no keys. I crept around the corner of the island and ran my hands over the surface once more, hoping maybe I'd missed them in the first go-over. Then, like a pit bull barking in the house, there was the same sound of someone pounding on the front door: *BANG! BANG! BANG!* Yet this time, it seemed louder than before.

I paused. My reflexes told me to run to the door and yank it open, but my mind was hesitant. The flushing toilet, the running faucets, the lights turning on and off and the sense that someone else was in the house just made me want to leave. Yet, it occurred to me that whoever had perpetrated those goings-on might be the same person knocking on the door. I wasn't sure I wanted to tangle with that person outside the house either. I also considered the possibility that someone inside was working with someone outside in a concerted effort to scare me out of the home. If so, it was working.

As these thoughts pin-balled in my head, there was more pounding: *BANG! BANG! BANG!* Loud, hard, insistent banging, like that of detectives on TV crime dramas when pounding on a suspect's door. It won me over: I didn't know who was out there, but the persistence of the knocking was too difficult to resist. I ran back to the front door. Again I fingered the locks trying to disengage them, and while doing so, there was another explosion of knocking: *BANG! BANG! BANG!* It rattled the whole door, and, it seemed, the whole house.

"I'm coming! I'm coming!" I shouted through the wood at the frantic knocker. I still wanted to believe it was a neighbor seeking help. At that point, I would have done anything for a neighbor in need just for the chance to bring some company into the house. The locks jumped back, I grabbed the brass knob and, though it was swollen from all the humidity, I tugged the door loose from its frame. There was no one on the other side.

I was in disbelief. Literally two seconds before, the wood of the door was shaking from the beating, and now not a soul was in sight. I went out into the middle of the walkway.

"HELLO?! HELLO?! *HELLO?!*" I shouted. I looked both ways up and down the side of the house and saw no one. The gate was shut as it had been before, and from what portion of the wall of the house I could see, nobody was pressed up against it hiding. Again I called into night: "Hello? Is anybody there?" Whoever had been knocking did not answer.

I was officially freaked out. I was determined to get away from the faucets, the lights, the knocking and the darkness. My resolve to go back in the house, get the car keys and spend the night elsewhere was renewed. I didn't care about possible explanations anymore; I just knew I'd had enough.

Back in the house, I slammed the door and locked it. If there was a creep outside, I wasn't about to leave unimpeded access into the home. I bolted up the steps to the second floor. By then my eyes had had more than enough time to adjust to the darkness, and the evolution of my unease into fear had me adrenalized. I found my pants on the chaise in the corner of the bedroom, and sure enough, my keys were in the left front pocket. Mentally I sighed with relief, but as I snatched the keys, more pounding punctuated the air: *BANG! BANG! BANG!*

At that point, my plan was not changing. I had the keys to the car, which meant I could leave; that was all I cared about at that moment. I knew I could sort it all out in the morning, but I also knew that I would *not* be waiting for morning in that house. I returned to the stairs—*BANG! BANG! BANG!*—and descended them quickly but carefully as not to somersault my way down the hard steps. Just as my foot touched down on the bottom step, again I heard echoing through the house: *BANG! BANG! BANG!*

I had to make a choice. I knew I had to go out the door and through the yard to get to my car, but I also realized that whoever was doing the pounding was probably hiding in that same yard. Determined not to stay in the dark, empty house a moment longer, it was decided.

Once again, the door shook: *BANG! BANG! BANG!* This time I didn't fumble with the locks. First the upper sprung back, and then the lower sprung back. I took the knob and opened the door.

"Sir? Sir, are you okay?" I could hear a woman's voice, and someone was shaking my shoulder. I opened my eyes, and sunlight flooded them, blinding me for a moment. I squinted up at the source of the voice, a woman of about forty years old. She was leaning over me with her hand still grasping my shoulder, but she had stopped shaking when I opened my eyes.

"Are you all right?" she said.

"Uh," I stammered, "I think so. I think so. What time is it?"

"It's 8:00 a.m.," she replied. As my eyes focused and adjusted to the immense brightness of the morning, I was able to make out more of the woman's appearance. It looked as if she was in her workout clothes. She had on colorful sneakers and was holding an iPod in her right, non-shoulder-shaking hand.

"I was just jogging and saw you passed out here on the sidewalk. Are you okay?" she said. Still groggy from sleep and confused about where I was and how I'd gotten there, I didn't know what to say. Physically, at least, I felt like I was in one piece. I took a moment to look around and get my bearings and gathered I was sitting, of all places, on the waterfront sidewalk that circled the Battery. My back was up against one of the many concrete pillars bracing thick iron rails, and my legs stuck out in front of me, obstructing the use of that half of the sidewalk. I must have looked like a drunk or a homeless man, or both. I turned my head to the left and could see that already there were a handful of runners, cyclists and tourists moving up and down the sidewalk. I wondered how long I'd been there and how many people had already passed me.

"I think I'm okay," I said, turning back to look her in the face. "I think I just fell asleep here, but I feel okay. Thank you."

"No problem. Just wanted to make sure." She smiled, put her earbuds back in and started jogging down the sidewalk.

Using the rail for support, I pulled myself up off the ground. I looked out over the water of the harbor. It was a beautiful morning. The blue sky was sprinkled with a few wispy clouds, the sun glinted off the surface of the water, and a few yards out two seagulls floated on the air, looking for a place to land. Aside from the residual dampness on the stones of the sidewalk, one would not have guessed that a few hours earlier a storm was raging. Regrettably, though, I could not recall the time that had elapsed between the storm and the blue skies.

I looked down at myself. I still had on the athletic shorts and white undershirt that I'd had on in the middle of the night. Yet they were dry; not soaked from the storm, through which, I suspected, I had run. Remembering my keys, I grabbed for my pockets and found them tucked there undisturbed. Though the sunlight made the previous night's chilling events seem like a distant memory or even a bad dream, I could not keep them from surfacing in my mind. I didn't want to, but I knew I had to go back to the house.

I looked across the street at the big, storybook-like houses on East Bay Street and could see I was directly across from the corner of East Bay and Georgian Street. If I had made a run from the house, I hadn't made it far. Without further hesitation, I walked down to the street and made my way back toward 44 Georgian.

The closer I got, the more my grogginess faded and the more I could remember from the night before. I recalled my decision to flee, but I could not remember anything beyond unlocking the front door that third time. How I had ended up unconscious beside the water was beyond me. My unease grew as I approached the home.

I took a right and followed the alley that led to the house's abbreviated driveway. The car, at least, was right where I'd parked it. It was plastered with leaves from the previous night's storm, but otherwise it appeared unharmed. Whoever—or whatever—had played on my nerves all evening had not, it appeared, been interested in auto theft. Having confirmed that, I knew I had to face the house.

I passed through the gate in the wrought-iron fence, and as I did, I saw that the yard surrounding the house was covered in debris. I hurried my pace toward the home and the debris and realized I was looking at my own luggage scattered all over the yard. Socks, shirts, boxers, blue jeans—everything I'd packed for the trip was scattered across the lawn. My black duffel bag was facing down in the wet grass. I kicked it over with my foot and could see every pocket had been unzipped and every item had been taken out. I leaned over and picked up a nearby t-shirt. It was sopping. As I stood there holding it, a small stream of water dripped off the fabric's bottom corner. Though I should have been angry at seeing my possessions soaked, stained and strewn all over the place, at that moment I was just mystified.

"Who would do this?" I thought. I let the wet shirt fall back to the ground and looked over at the house. Through the windows I could see there were no visible lights on illuminating the interior of the home. I moved from the yard onto the brick patio.

As I peered through the windows, there was no sign of motion in the house. Rather, from what I could tell, the inside just looked still and quiet. I followed the brick pathway, also plastered with leaves, to the stoop in front of the door. I looked at the surface of the door. There was no evidence of the pounding that had rattled it just a short time before. I reached for the door's brass knob, turned it and pushed. Nothing. The door was locked.

That was good enough for me. I turned on the stoop, walked down the two brick steps and headed back for the yard. Perhaps if the house had been unlocked I would have gone inside and looked around, but after all that had happened, when I found the place locked up either by my hand or another's, I took it as a sign not to go back in the old, three-story home.

In the yard, I collected my things. Though they were wet, muddy and sprinkled with leaves, I shoved everything back in my duffel bag and made my way toward the car. I unlocked the trunk and threw inside the dripping bag. With the house locked, my luggage in my possession and the keys to my getaway car in hand, I was content to leave.

I opened the driver's-side door and sat down behind the wheel. The rain had cooled the outside air, which had, in turn, fogged up the interior of the car's windows. I didn't pay any attention to the phenomenon until I was in the driver's seat and, out of habit, immediately inserted the key into the ignition and started the car. The air-conditioning kicked on automatically. The cool air coming out of the vents rolled up the sides of the windows and the windshield, evaporating the thin fog on the inside of the car. Within a second or two, the conditioned air completely cleared the inside of the glass.

Before it could, however, I looked up from putting the key in the ignition and read these words fingered into the foggy residue on the inside of the windshield: *DON'T COME BACK.* In a moment the fog and the message were gone. For a second, perhaps, I hesitated, but then I put the car in drive, pulled out of the driveway and never returned to 44 Georgian Street again.

BIBLIOGRAPHY

Bower, Jennifer Bean. *Winston & Salem: Tales of Murder, Mystery and Mayhem.* Charleston, SC: The History Press, 2007.

Calloway, Burt, and Jennifer FitzSimons. *Triad Hauntings.* Winston-Salem, NC: Bandit Books, 1990.

Casstevens, Frances H. *Ghosts of the North Carolina Piedmont.* Charleston, SC: The History Press, 2009.

www.digitalforsyth.org. The official website of Digital Forsyth.

www.examiner.com/historic-places-in-winstonsalem/guy-montgomery. The Winston-Salem Historic Places Examiner page.

www.findagrave.com. The official website of Find a Grave.

www.oldsalem.org. The official website of Old Salem Museums and Gardens.

Roberts, Nancy. *North Carolina Ghosts and Legends.* Columbia: University of South Carolina Press, 1991.

www.salem.edu. The official website of Salem College.

Starbuck, Richard W. *Ghosts of Salem and Other Tales.* Winston-Salem, NC: Moravian Archives, 2002.

www.theshadowlands.net. The official website of Shadowlands Haunted Places Index.

About the Author

Photograph by Kathy Miller Hawkins.

G.T. Montgomery is a graduate of Wake Forest University, from which he received a degree in English literature. He worked for Old Salem Museums and Gardens, the living history museum that works to preserve Old Salem, from 2009 through 2012. He now resides back in his hometown of Louisville, Kentucky, with his wife, Genevieve, and their two dogs and cat. *Ghosts of Old Salem, North Carolina* is his first book.

www.ingramcontent.com/pod-product-compliance
Lightning Source LLC
Chambersburg PA
CBHW060813100426
42813CB00004B/1061